NEW DIRECTIONS FOR EVALUATION
A Publication of the American Evaluation Association

Gary T. Henry, *Georgia State University*
EDITOR-IN-CHIEF

Jennifer C. Greene, *Cornell University*
EDITOR-IN-CHIEF

Realist Evaluation: An Emerging Theory in Support of Practice

Gary T. Henry
Georgia State University

George Julnes
University of Illinois-Springfield

Melvin M. Mark
The Pennsylvania State University

EDITORS

Number 78, Summer 1998

JOSSEY-BASS PUBLISHERS
San Francisco

REALIST EVALUATION: AN EMERGING THEORY IN SUPPORT OF PRACTICE
Gary T. Henry, George Julnes, Melvin M. Mark (eds.)
New Directions for Evaluation, no. 78
Jennifer C. Greene, Gary T. Henry, Editors-in-Chief

Microfilm copies of issues and articles are available in 16mm and 35mm, as well as microfiche in 105mm, through University Microfilms Inc., 300 North Zeeb Road, Ann Arbor, Michigan 48106–1346.

New Directions for Evaluation is indexed in Contents Pages in Education, Higher Education Abstracts, and Sociological Abstracts.

ISSN 1097-6736   ISBN 0-7879-1551-3

NEW DIRECTIONS FOR EVALUATION is part of The Jossey-Bass Education Series and is published quarterly by Jossey-Bass Inc., Publishers, 350 Sansome Street, San Francisco, California 94104–1342.

SUBSCRIPTIONS cost $63.00 for individuals and $105.00 for institutions, agencies, and libraries. Prices subject to change.

EDITORIAL CORRESPONDENCE should be addressed to the Editors-in-Chief, Jennifer C. Greene, Department of Policy Analysis and Management, MVR Hall, Cornell University, Ithaca, NY 14853–4401, or Gary T. Henry, School of Policy Studies, Georgia State University, P.O. Box 4039, Atlanta, GA 30302–4039.

www.josseybass.com

Printed in the United States of America on Lyons Falls Turin Book. This paper is acid-free and 100 percent totally chlorine-free.

EDITORIAL POLICY AND PROCEDURES

New Directions for Evaluation, a quarterly sourcebook, is an official publication of the American Evaluation Association. The journal publishes empirical, methodological, and theoretical works on all aspects of evaluation. A reflective approach to evaluation is an essential strand to be woven through every volume. The editors encourage volumes that have one of three foci: (1) craft volumes that present approaches, methods, or techniques that can be applied in evaluation practice, such as the use of templates, case studies, or survey research; (2) professional issue volumes that present issues of import for the field of evaluation, such as utilization of evaluation or locus of evaluation capacity; (3) societal issue volumes that draw out the implications of intellectual, social, or cultural developments for the field of evaluation, such as the women's movement, communitarianism, or multiculturalism. A wide range of substantive domains is appropriate for *New Directions for Evaluation;* however, the domains must be of interest to a large audience within the field of evaluation. We encourage a diversity of perspectives and experiences within each volume, as well as creative bridges between evaluation and other sectors of our collective lives.

The editors do not consider or publish unsolicited single manuscripts. Each issue of the journal is devoted to a single topic, with contributions solicited, organized, reviewed, and edited by a guest editor. Issues may take any of several forms, such as a series of related chapters, a debate, or a long article followed by brief critical commentaries. In all cases, the proposals must follow a specific format, which can be obtained from the editor-in-chief. These proposals are sent to members of the editorial board and to relevant substantive experts for peer review. The process may result in acceptance, a recommendation to revise and resubmit, or rejection. However, the editors are committed to working constructively with potential guest editors to help them develop acceptable proposals.

Jennifer C. Greene, Editor-in-Chief
Department of Policy Analysis and Management
MVR Hall
Cornell University
Ithaca, NY 14853–4401
e-mail: jcg8@cornell.edu

Gary T. Henry, Editor-in-Chief
School of Policy Studies
Georgia State University
P.O. Box 4039
Atlanta, GA 30302–4039
e-mail: gthenry@gsu.edu

CONTENTS

EDITORS' NOTES

Several years ago, we began a collaborative project to develop a theory of evaluation grounded in realist principles and informed by decades of practice in the field. In realism, we saw a largely neglected paradigm that could be useful for evaluation as well as for other forms of social research. We were not the first to see this potential. Donald Campbell, Ernie House, Thomas Cook, and more recently our British colleagues, Nick Tilley and Ray Pawson, have found promise in the realist school of the philosophy of science. In this sourcebook, you will find their influences, but we have labored to provide a more comprehensive treatment than has been previously available.

Why is another theory of evaluation needed? The "paradigm wars" have left a void in their wake. A new theory, firmly grounded in a credible philosophy of science, is needed to guide practice. Our aim is to provide a new theory that captures the sensemaking contributions from post-positivism and the sensitivity to values from constructivist traditions. The theory presented here is not a slap-dash synthesis of the competing paradigms—it is a new approach. Some of the contributions of the realist theory of evaluation are (1) providing a basis for principled discovery as we oscillate between explanations and data; (2) using explanation as a means for extrapolating findings from one evaluation to other settings; (3) viewing all methods, both quantitative and qualitative, as aids to sensemaking that have strengths and flaws; (4) connecting evaluation practice with the ultimate goal of most program evaluation—social betterment; and (5) balancing the focus of the evaluation between sensemaking and value inquiry.

This sourcebook is organized around the five-component framework for evaluation theory set out in Shadish, Cook, and Leviton (1991). We begin with a chapter by Mark, Henry, and Julnes that overviews our vision of realist evaluation practice by presenting a running conversation and a sample preproposal that illustrates many of the basic principles of emergent realist evaluation. Next, Julnes and Mark trace the history of realism and its implications for knowledge construction in the field of evaluation. In Chapter Three, Henry and Julnes give a perspective on values that links evaluation to social progress and provides a "seat at the table" for traditional stakeholders and the public. Next, Mark and Henry review theory and research on social policy-making and programming in Chapter Four and draw implications for the practice of evaluation. In Chapter Five, Henry and Rog place the use of evaluation findings in the context of the development of social policies and programs, and they formulate a balanced perspective on the potential for evaluation information. Finally, the Epilogue assesses where we are in our quest to provide a theory that both assists the development of practice and is informed by practice.

NEW DIRECTIONS FOR EVALUATION, no. 78, Summer 1998 © Jossey-Bass Publishers

1

In attempting to set out what we firmly believe is a new direction for evaluation within the constraints of a sourcebook, we provide a broad, but abbreviated, summary. Many of the references elaborate our arguments. In addition, we will be providing a more complete treatment of this theory, including topics that space limitations prevent us from addressing here, in a co-authored book that is well under way (Mark, Henry, and Julnes, in preparation). In that book, we will take a broader view of evaluation than in past realist efforts. For example, more attention will be given to monitoring and classification.

References

Mark, M. M., Henry, G. T., and Julnes, G. "Evaluation, A Realist Approach: Monitoring, Classification, Causal Analysis, and Values Inquiry," in preparation.

Shadish, W. R., Cook, T. D., and Leviton, L. C. *Foundations of Program Evaluation: Theories of Practice.* Newberry, Calif.: Sage, 1991.

GARY T. HENRY *is professor of policy studies and political science at Georgia State University.*

GEORGE JULNES *is Visiting Research Specialist at the Institute for Public Affairs, University of Illinois at Springfield.*

MELVIN M. MARK *is professor of psychology at Pennsylvania State University.*

Some of the essential points of applying emergent realist theory to practice are sketched in this chapter. First a running conversation is offered to explain emergent realist evaluation; then an example pre-proposal highlights important aspects of practice.

A Realist Theory of Evaluation Practice

Melvin M. Mark, Gary T. Henry, George Julnes

It is by imagination that we can form any conception of what are his sensations.
Adam Smith, *Theory of Moral Sentiments* (2nd ed.), 1762

It was just my imagination, once again, running away with me.
The Temptations (Norman Whitfield and Barrett Strong, songwriters, 1971)

In this chapter and in those that follow, we present a realist theory of evaluation. Realism is a tradition of increasing importance in evaluation (House, 1991; Pawson and Tilley, 1997), and we refer to our approach as emergent realism. Shadish, Cook, and Leviton (1991) list practice as the last of the five components of evaluation theory; the other four components provide the *terra firma* on which practice is constructed. For example, the knowledge construction component (see Julnes and Mark, Chapter Two) serves as the foundation for choices about research methods. But we have chosen in this sourcebook to bring the practice component to the forefront. This provides the best distillation of emergent realist theory in that it both introduces and summarizes the other components. By beginning this sourcebook with the practice component, we hope to introduce many of the most salient characteristics of emergent realist evaluation (ERE) theory and to show how ERE differs from other theories of evaluation. This discussion of practice, however, is based on emergent realist principles elaborated more fully later in this volume.

To better form a concept of what ERE is, we ask you, the reader, to exercise your imagination by placing yourself in the role of an emergent realist evaluator and considering how an emergent realist views a variety of questions that arise in the practice of evaluation.

As you prepare to leave the house, you, the emergent realist evaluator, think about the meeting you have scheduled today with a fellow evaluator to talk about collaborating on a proposal for an evaluation of a state program for preschoolers. You think the two of you can use emergent realist ideas to frame the proposal, but you need to introduce your colleague to emergent realism. You think you might say something like. . . .

Emergent realist evaluation, or ERE, is an approach to evaluation based both on a philosophy called neo-realism and on an integration of lessons drawn by many evaluators from practice, theory, and research. Like other forms of realism, emergent realism assumes that reality exists apart from our understanding of it. Emergent realists believe, to take a timeworn example, that if a tree fell in a forest, its crash would create the sound waves that could be registered as sound, even if no one were there to hear it. While this might seem like an obvious assumption, it actually differs from the idealism held by some constructivists who deny that there is any reality apart from our interpretations. Emergent realism also assumes, as do most forms of realism, that there are regular patterns in the world that we can detect, including *underlying generative mechanisms.* When we observe an event—say, a tree falling in the forest—the event is caused by unobserved processes, such as gravity, that occur at other levels. Although gravity, as an underlying mechanism, is not itself directly observable, it has detectable consequences, such as the falling of a tree. Similarly, the crashing of the tree makes detectable sounds because of underlying regularities involving sound waves and their impact on the human ear. Unobservable underlying mechanisms give rise to observable events.

Reality, then, is hierarchical or stratified, in the sense that there are molecular, reductionistic levels (such as gravity and airwaves) and molar, holistic levels (such as trees falling and producing detectable sounds). In general, entities at the more molecular levels, such as gravity, are referred to as underlying generative mechanisms or structures, while those at the more molar levels, such as falling trees, are referred to as events and, when they are actually observed, as experiences.

There are other aspects of the emergent realist approach that it would be nice to convey, you think, such as the concept of "emergent properties" and "open systems," but this is already too deep for a morning meeting about writing a proposal. Maybe later. But you'd better mention, early on, a bit on the ERE perspective on sensemaking and valuing.

Emergent realists also assume that, as complex organisms in the world, humans have evolved sensemaking capabilities for understanding the world. For example, humans have evolved the ability to hear sounds that correspond to certain wavelengths. Unlike so-called naive realists, emergent realists assume that these evolved sensemaking capabilities, although adaptive, are imperfect—

they are indirect, constrained, and influenced by past experience. For example, one might "hear" a tree falling when no tree actually fell because of expectations, visual cues, and background noise. Emergent realists also recognize that, in addition to biologically evolved sensemaking processes, there are socially constructed sensemaking technologies designed to supplement the biological processes. For instance, one might use a hearing aid to better hear falling trees, conduct an experiment to better estimate the effects of some intervention, or carry out a survey to gather information from a larger and more representative set of individuals than one person could readily observe or interview. With critical realists, emergent realists bring a critical perspective to the assessment of the quality of these constructed technologies as an aid to evolved sensemaking. While constructed technologies *may* improve understanding, each one is fallible, and its limitations should be analyzed in the specific context in which it is used. The ERE perspective on evaluation methods, then, is that they are constructed technologies, to be used—with critical analysis of their value *in situ*—to help in making sense about social programs.

But ERE sees sensemaking as just one of the two prongs of evaluation. *(In fact, one key difference you saw between emergent realism and previous theories of evaluation—a difference that drew you to emergent realism—is its dual focus on sensemaking and valuing.)* Prior to ERE, most realist efforts emphasized only sensemaking. For example, Campbell, a sophisticated critical realist, emphasized the use of techniques designed to estimate the impact of programs. This is a form of sensemaking whereby the evaluator intervenes in the world, through the use of research design and measuring instruments, with the goal of better understanding aspects of the world (specifically, the program's effects). In contrast, some theorists, such as Guba and Lincoln (1989), focus more on addressing the value issues surrounding programs. ERE in a real sense represents a third alternative that focuses on both sensemaking and value-probing.

The emphasis on values in ERE serves partly as a counterweight to the inadequate attention historically given to values in the experimentalist tradition in evaluation, and partly as an explicit recognition of the value-laden context within which evaluations are conducted. For example, an evaluation of a social program or policy can rarely measure all of the possible consequences, intended and unintended, that each stakeholder group and the public values. But by measuring those outcomes that are related to some groups' value positions, an evaluation will legitimate those values, while giving short shrift to others. Emerging realist (ER) evaluators explicitly recognize that different individuals and groups assign varying levels of importance to different values, and that choices made in the evaluation process can serve some value perspectives and the parties that hold them over others. In addition, ER evaluators believe that the value positions surrounding social programs can and should be directly studied, and it is this belief that differentiates the ERE position on values from many other approaches to evaluation.

The issues concerning values are tricky, but enough for now. The general point you'll need to make up front is that ERE consciously addresses both sensemaking activities, such as estimating the effects of programs, and valuing activities, such as assessing whose values are served by particular outcome patterns. And you know that your colleague is an experienced and savvy evaluator, who is well aware of the value conflicts that can arise in the design of evaluations and in the utilization of evaluation findings, so you expect her to be receptive to your points about values. But you'll have a limited amount of time to meet and discuss your prospective collaboration. And you expect that one of the first things she's going to ask, if you push your ERE perspective, is what difference ERE makes in terms of how you will frame the evaluation. So, as you drive to the meeting, you think about. . . .

How does an adherent of ERE specify priorities among the various purposes that evaluation might serve? Of the many purposes that evaluations might have, what is generally most important? And how might the particular circumstances of a given evaluation lead to different priorities?

Although a more nuanced and contingent realist view of evaluation is forthcoming (Mark, Henry, and Julnes, in preparation), realist evaluation to date (House, 1991; Pawson and Tilley, 1997) has given general priority to explanation, in the sense of identifying (1) the manipulable generative mechanisms that underlie program effects, and (2) the conditions under which these mechanisms operate, including (3) the types of individuals for whom they operate. This approach, if it works properly, serves three functions of evaluation: formative, summative, and knowledge construction (Scriven, 1990; Patton, 1997).

As you think about this point, you try to recall one of your favorite quotes from Lee Cronbach, who was one of the first and foremost advocates of explanation as a focus of evaluation. In the quote, Cronbach indicates the desired overlap of formative and summative evaluation and knowledge construction. If you could recall the quote verbatim, you would remember it as

> Evaluation that focuses on outcomes can and should be used formatively. When a trial fails, the social planner wants to know why it failed and how to do better next time. When the trial succeeds and the proposal is considered for use under changed conditions, the intelligent planner does not conclude that its effectiveness has been proved. She now asks about the reasons and essential conditions for the success. Even when the trial of a plan has satisfactory outcomes, the policy maker should be prepared to consider any alternative that has a chance of working appreciably better (Cronbach, 1982, p. 12).

So a focus on underlying generative mechanisms aids formative purposes by providing a basis for strengthening an intervention, making it more efficient, better targeting it to those who will be most helped, and designing future interventions—all of which are easier to do if you understand *why* a program works. Learning about underlying mechanisms also serves traditional objectives of summative evaluation. In particular, knowledge of generative mechanisms is a valuable basis for generalizations about the likely effectiveness of the program for other persons, settings, or times (Cronbach, 1982; Mark, 1990; Cook, 1993). In addition, studying underlying mechanisms requires assessing the effects of a program, usually on multiple outcomes. Thus, the emergent realist's focus on underlying mechanisms will also typically provide information about the merit or worth of the program, in the sense advocated by Scriven (1990).

Another car cuts into your lane, causing you to turn your full attention to driving. As you get back to thinking about your meeting, you realize that your colleague will probably push you on ERE's focus on explanation. You can hear her ask: Should every evaluation focus on underlying mechanisms? Aren't there areas where we have social programs but lack the substantive knowledge needed to develop good explanations? And sometimes aren't there important evaluation tasks that should be done that don't involve explanation? You plot your reply. . . .

Although emergent realist evaluation places a priority on research that probes underlying mechanisms, it does not hold that *all* evaluation should be of this form. When interventions are new and rapidly evolving, especially when the intervention and/or evaluation resources are small, it may be preferable to do more formative evaluation work, such as evaluability assessment (Wholey, 1987). Moreover, some interventions are "puny," as illustrated by the one-hour speaker approach to diversity training or sexual assault awareness prevalent on some college campuses. Mechanism-probing evaluation research is typically labor and resource intensive. While it should be helpful to look at puny interventions through an ERE lens, it is probably not cost-effective to evaluate them with a full scale mechanism-probing study.

Moreover, explanation can sometimes take place at a relatively molar level. (See an extended discussion of this issue in Chapter Two.) While emergent realists emphasize the value of explanation, they also insist, first, that explanation occurs at different levels and, second, that a highly molar explanation, containing simply the description of the causal relationship, can be important and useful. Human history is filled with cases in which people recognized and used regularities without a satisfactory molecular explanation. Pre-industrial humans recognized many toxic substances and developed rules of diet and, in some cases, practices such as using poison darts for hunting, without an adequate explanation of the underlying physiological processes. People have long used electricity and aspirin without good explanations for their effects. Similarly, the harmful average effects of smoking have been recognized without a satisfactory account of the mechanism by which it operates. Indeed, individuals and social groups can be right about useful causal regularities while holding an incorrect explanatory account. For example, manipulation of the spine by a chiropractor is effective for lower back pain; fortunately, we do not have to believe chiropractic theory, which holds that virtually all medical problems arise from spinal misalignment, to take advantage of this effect (Carey and others, 1995). In short, although a good account of underlying mechanisms is valuable and often leads to more efficient or more effective action, it is also possible to have useful knowledge about causal regularities without having a molecular explanation. Sometimes knowing an average effect size, for the specific contexts in which a program operates, is good enough for decision-making for the time being, as manipulability theorists (Shadish, Cook, and Leviton, 1991) such as Campbell have argued. Thus, though emergent realist evaluators aspire to good molecular explanations as a goal of evaluation, they also believe the position held by manipulability theorists can be a useful fallback, at least if one can be confident about the applicability of the findings in the particular context(s) of interest. In short, when the level of knowledge is not adequate for testing explanatory accounts of underlying mechanisms, ERE endorses research that (1) allows more molar causal assertions about the effects of a program, with emphasis on identifying the conditions under which particular effects occur, and (2) helps develop knowledge about underlying mechanisms.

Viewed from a developmental perspective on knowledge construction, an emergent realist approach to evaluation involves seeking a relatively complete account of underlying mechanisms, but with the realization that such accounts may *emerge* over time and research efforts. ER evaluators should not, however, require or expect a detailed, empirically supported explanatory account for all actions or all recommendations (see, for example, House, 1991, on the Mackie's analysis of causal relations). Good evidence about program effects may suffice for judgments of merit and worth, even if explanation is molar or lacking. But less confidence will be warranted in generalizations to other sites or in formative suggestions about program improvements, relative to the degree of confidence one could have if better knowledge about mechanisms were available.

You think about making one other point about those evaluation activities that do not involve explanation: Contemporary realists are concerned not only with underlying generative mechanisms, but also with underlying structures or categories. Many evaluation tasks can be analyzed in terms of this focus, but the development of ERE to date has emphasized sensemaking with respect to underlying mechanisms (see Chapter Two; for a more comprehensive account of realist evaluation, including a description of classification and other evaluation tasks to carry out when explanation is of less interest, see Mark, Henry, and Julnes, in preparation). "So enough about explanation and sensemaking already," you imagine your colleague saying, "What about this values piece of ERE you mentioned?"

In addition to the more familiar knowledge construction purposes, a major purpose of ER evaluation is to unpack the value issues surrounding a program. ERE sees values-probing as a core focus of evaluation activity, in conjunction with the sensemaking activities that center on estimating program effects, assessing contextual determinants of success, and probing underlying mechanisms. Values are important throughout the life cycle of programs, from the definition of a social condition as a social problem, to the selection of program alternatives, to the decision about whether to initiate a particular program, to decisions about whether to continue, expand, or modify a program. Values influence evaluation use. Entrenched—but typically implicit—value positions in the "policy setting community" (Cronbach, 1982; Kingdon, 1995) can prevent evaluation from sparking program improvements. In part this occurs because stakeholders may draw conclusions about programs based on value positions that are relatively resistant to information about effects (Ross and Nisbett, 1991). For example, in the treatment of homeless individuals in the United States, some people are committed to the building of dwellings in residential neighborhoods not because of any evidence that these result in better outcomes, but because they see it as a matter of human dignity and decency. Others respond, "Not in my backyard" to the construction of shelters, regardless of any evidence about the impact of such shelters on crime, property values, or any other outcomes (Wright, 1991). In short, evidence about program effects, even evidence about underlying mechanisms, may fail to influence the conclusions stakeholders will draw because values can overcome the effect of evidence. In addition, those involved in debates and decisions about programs (elected officials, for example) are often influenced by assumptions about the values held by others (such as constituents). Thus, evaluation can inform policy processes by addressing such questions as "What sort of outcome pattern satisfies whose values?"

Unlike Guba and Lincoln (1989), ERE does not view the evaluator as the necessary vehicle for negotiating value discrepancies. But ERE does acknowledge that policy-making and social programming are not based solely on information about underlying mechanisms. Evaluations may be more potent—at least in the sense of stimulating discourse—when they also provide information about which outcomes, generated by which mechanisms, are valued by whom. Of course, as with other social phenomena, the emergent realist evaluator recognizes that values may be affected by context and are susceptible to change over time—which may have implications for the assessment of values and the reporting of findings about them.

As you make the last turn approaching the meeting site, you imagine your colleague's next comment. You know she's read Shadish, Cook, and Leviton (1991) and will point out that, even when the general purpose of an evaluation is determined, choices are likely to remain about which specific questions to address. If, for example, one's purpose is to estimate the effects of a program, the issue of question choice arises in terms of how to decide which of the many possible effects one should measure. You think about this as you approach the building.

Question choice for the mechanism-probing brand of ER evaluation is, in one sense, quite simple. Evaluators should address those research questions that help identify which mechanisms are operating and which are not. For example, if the addition of a given dependent variable will help differentiate between two possible mechanisms, it is important to add measures of this variable. For instance, Entwisle (1995) indicates that, in research on the long-term social effects of preschool programs, one possible mechanism is that preschool participation allows some of the participants to avoid negative tracking, such as placement in lower-level reading groups or retention in the early grades. In evaluating a preschool program, then, this potential underlying mechanism could be probed by assessing the impact of preschool participation on tracking assignments. Question choice is based on program theory, then, and the evaluator will typically focus on estimating effects relevant to program theory, as well as on testing potential moderators and mediators of these effects. For example, the effect of preschool could be moderated by the quality of the schools the preschool participants enter (Lee and Loeb, 1995).

However, other criteria may also often be needed to guide question choice. In some cases, for example, only a few outcome measures will be needed to differentiate among alternative mechanisms, and another criterion will be needed to select among the other possible measures. In other cases, the knowledge base in a particular area may be inadequate for a strong, molecular search for underlying mechanisms, and some other criterion may be needed to select among possible measures. On what basis, then, other than importance for testing mechanisms, should the evaluator select among the many possible effects? The ERE answer, put simply, is that the evaluator should select, first, those effects that reflect the public's interest in the program and, second, those that are important to other important stakeholders.

For ER evaluators in particular, another issue arises with respect to question choice: At what level of molecularity should we seek explanatory accounts? Explanations for a social program's effects can be given at different levels of analysis, from the neurological to the psychological to the social-structural. From this perspective, ERE replaces the metaphor of the program as a black box to be explored with the more apt metaphor of a set of Russian stacking dolls, where another level of explanation always underlies whatever level we are examining. ERE does not call for evaluators to move inexorably on to more molecular levels of analysis. While such an approach might be appropriate for basic research, it is impractical in the applied world of evaluation. Instead, utilization serves as a practical determinant of how far to go within the set of nested dolls. For example, there would be no reason to move from a psychological to a neurological level of analysis, unless doing so could reasonably lead to better agenda setting, selection of alternatives, choice of an alternative, or implementation activities (see Henry and Rog, Chapter Five).

A similar concern arises in terms of how far evaluators should go in looking for additional contextual determinants of program success. Testing alternative mechanisms often involves looking for moderators, that is, for contextual and client factors that change program effectiveness. (In statistical terms, this involves testing for significant interactions between the program and client or contextual factors). For example, a treatment program for homeless substance abusers might be found to be ineffective for homeless who have a psychological disorder, but effective for others. But a focus on client and contextual boundaries can lead researchers into Cronbach's (1975) "infinite hall of mirrors," whereby we encounter ever higher-order interactions that limit the initial lower-level contextual interactions. For example, the interaction between the homelessness intervention and client psychopathology might take place in a higher-order interaction, such that the treatment is effective for homeless without a psychological disorder only at sites where other social services are adequate. The molar-molecular dimension also applies to the study of inter-actions. The focus on increasingly higher-order interactions can be seen as mol-ecular—at its extreme, focusing on the response of each individual in a single setting—relative to the molar main-effect approach involved in examining only the average effect of the treatment relative to the control group. Some scholars (such as Guba and Lincoln, 1989) have reacted to the possibility that a find-ing might be limited by higher-order interactions by insisting on highly mol-ecular analyses and, further, by denying the utility and even the existence of social regularities. ERE is not sympathetic to this stand which, as its critics note, is embedded in a radical relativism which leaves us with no warrant for any action (for example, see Pawson and Tilley, 1997). The question remains, though, of how to choose the level of molecularity to be employed in our explanatory accounts. ERE suggests that the level of molecularity should be driven by (1) utility, so that explanations are at a level corresponding to the needs and conceptions of those who will use an evaluation, and (2) empirical evidence, regarding the large (and policy-relevant) contextual determinants that need to be accounted for so that the explanatory account is a useful guide to practice.

You park your car, grab your briefcase, and head inside. After greetings, the meeting begins. To your surprise, it begins pretty much as you expected. The one thing you hadn't had time to think about in advance, of course, turns out to be the one thing that your colleague is really interested in—the issue of "method choice." That is, what guidance does ERE provide on how to select the research methods for a particular evaluation? In trying to be concise, you discuss this issue a bit mechanically.

The primary criterion for method choice for sensemaking, according to ERE, is the method's suitability for probing underlying mechanisms. ER dis-tinguishes between two general approaches to the study of underlying mech-anisms: (1) *competitive elaboration,* which can be applied when alternative generative mechanisms are articulated in advance, and (2) *principled discovery,* which can be applied when generative mechanisms are not adequately speci-fied in advance. In fact, competitive elaboration and principled discovery share the same underlying logic, but the distinction is useful in practice.

You decide to explain competitive elaboration first, both conceptually and in terms of methods that can be used to carry it out, even though principled discovery might be carried out first. Why hadn't you thought about method choice on the way over?

Competitive elaboration refers to the process by which alternative expla-nations—whether alternative program theories or validity threats—are ruled out (Reichardt and Mark, 1998). Competitive elaboration involves (a) speci-fying the implications of a possible mechanism to discover those that conflict with the implications of alternative mechanisms (including validity threats), and (b) obtaining data to see whether the implications of the mechanism or of its competitor hold true. In other words, when an explanatory account is sus-ceptible to alternative explanation, the plausibility of the alternative—and of the original—can be put to test by adding a comparison that creates competition between the explanatory account and the alternative explanation. The comparison can be made with respect to any of the elements of a causal relationship: cause, recipients, setting, time, and outcome variable (Reichardt and Mark, 1998). For preschool programs, Entwisle has articulated three potential generative mechanisms for the long-term effects that have been observed (1995; for descriptions of the effects, see Barnett, 1995; Consortium for Longitudinal Studies, 1992; McKey, 1985). The first possible mechanism is that increases in IQ score allow preschoolers to avoid negative tracking assignments, and the better tracking assignments in turn stimulate better outcomes. A second potential mechanism is that preschool participation causes parents, teachers, and others in the child's social world to hold higher expectations for the children, and the children respond to the enhanced socialization that results. According to the third of Entwisle's possible generative mechanisms, the preschool serves directly as a trigger to make the children ready for the rigors of kindergarten and first grade. Each mechanism specifies some short-term changes that can be measured and tested. In addition, an ER evaluator would be aware that each mechanism might work differently with children from different family and social environments. (For other examples, see Mark, 1990; Mark, Hofmann, and Reichardt, 1992; and Reichardt and Mark, 1998).

Competitive elaboration can be accomplished through a variety of research designs: (1) In the quantitative domain, moderated multiple regression, analysis of variance, or other techniques can be used in planned analyses to assess causal mechanisms by determining whether observed program effects are robust across different client subgroups, settings, outcome variables, treatment variations, and time lags. For example, in a well-known time series quasi-experiment, Ross, Campbell, and Glass (1970) found that a crackdown on drunken driving in Britain was followed by reduced traffic fatalities during the hours pubs were open, and that no such decline occurred in hours when pubs were closed. This pattern helped demonstrate that the crackdown reduced drunken driving, and it helped rule out a number of alternative explanations. Analyses that assess the robustness of program effects across subgroups, settings, outcomes, or time, even if not definitive in pointing to one mechanism over others, can be useful to policy-making in terms of showing possible limits to generalizability. (See Julnes, 1995; Mark, 1990; Mark, Hofmann, and Reichardt, 1992; and Reichardt and Mark, 1998, for examples and discussion of these and other benefits of this approach.) (2) Hierarchical linear modeling (HLM) and related techniques can be employed to study the effects of variables at different levels of aggregation (Bryk and Raudenbush, 1992). These techniques have been commonly used in education, for example, to examine the interactions of school-, classroom-, and pupil-level variables. HLM can be used, for instance, to investigate community-level effects and how they interact with program effects. (3) Meta-analyses can also provide evidence about moderated effects when a number of evaluation studies have been conducted (Cook and others, 1992; also see House, 1991, who argues for meta-analysis from a scientific realist perspective). (4) We can also learn about mechanisms through the study of mediation, which is another form of competitive elaboration whereby one's program theory predicts that the program's effect on an outcome will be mediated by some other variable, whereas alternative explanations do not make this prediction. For example, Seligman's revised theory of depression predicts that those in therapy will first show a change in the sort of causal attributions they give for negative events, and that the use of these attributions will statistically account for subsequent change in depression; alternative explanations do not make this prediction. (5) In some instances, as Pawson and Tilley (1997) point out, basic research will be informative about generative mechanisms in social programs. For example, Borkovec and Miranda (1996) use the results of laboratory experiments from cognitive psychology and other areas as part of the web of evidence to argue for their model of treatment for generalized anxiety disorder. (6) Qualitative methods can also be employed for competitive elaboration (Yin, 1994; Campbell, 1974; Maxwell, 1996; Mohr, 1995). For example, in a recent evaluation of the impact of a technology funding program on instructional processes, through case study methods a few specific mechanisms were identified as necessary but, by themselves, insufficient to stimulate an impact (Jones, Dolan, and Henry, 1996). On-site teacher training and availability of technical support for labs and classroom equipment, for instance, were found to be present in many situations where technology was most highly used. However, each component was also present in cases where the technology was not heavily used. The generative mechanisms underlying high use of technology were observed to take a varied, but not entirely unsystematic, route. In a follow-up study, ten sites are being used as case studies to further elaborate these mechanisms and to see if there are discernible packages or configurations that seem to lead to higher levels of instructional use and under what circumstances these configurations work. Smith (1997) presents a similar example that relies on the integration of qualitative and quantitative research. (7) More generally, competitive elaboration involves the use of pattern matching (Campbell, 1966; Trochim, 1985)—which can in fact encompass all the preceding approaches. For example, in an evaluation of Georgia's HOPE (college) scholarship program, Henry and Bugler (1997) hypothesized that the program's requirement of a B or better average in college and its limit of four years of support would serve as potential triggers for several outcomes: higher GPA, more credit hours earned, and greater likelihood of remaining in college after two years of study. Program impact was tested on a sample of marginally qualified students and on subgroups of traditionally underserved students, specifically African Americans and women. The HOPE scholars earned more credit hours, had higher GPAs, and were more likely to remain in college. However, this was true whether or not the HOPE scholars had retained their scholarships. This pattern of results is consistent with the interpretation that, underlying the HOPE program's effects, is a mechanism whereby it legitimizes scholarship recipients as college students (Gamoran, 1996).

"So," your colleague asks, "for competitive elaboration, you start with a program theory—or at least a hypothesis about an underlying mechanism, right? But what does ERE say you should do when you don't start with a good hypothesis about the underlying mechanism?" Ah, you reply, that's precisely what "principled discovery" is about—how to do elaboration in the absence of strong theory.

In many cases in which evaluations are done, theories may be inadequate. And having 100 equally speculative theories is probably no better as a guide to research than having none. Moreover, in some cases, programs are evaluated before practitioners are able to develop the experientially based theories that can guide realist evaluations. What do we do in these cases? How do we ask the data, rather than practitioners or social science theory, to provide the program theory to further guide us? There are several possible approaches. (1) The exploratory data analyses of Tukey (1977) and other graphical methods (Henry, 1995) could be used more widely to guide informed speculation about underlying mechanisms. Even if not predicted in advance, the observation that larger effects cluster in one subgroup, or in one setting, should set off additional investigation and the search for the underlying mechanism. (2) Techniques such as regression and analysis of covariance can be used in an exploratory fashion—and indeed may be most important as exploratory tools (Tukey, 1977)—to search for variations in treatment effectiveness across subgroups and settings. One approach is to use residuals to identify sites or cases that have larger or smaller outcomes than would be expected from standard predictors. These extreme cases can be contrasted to see if the variation in outcome appears to be associated with differences in types of participants or in treatment implementation, relying perhaps on qualitative data from interviews or observations. However, these and other efforts at discovery should be principled—-for example, evaluators should not present an interaction they stumbled upon as though it were the confirmation of a hypothesized mechanism. Rather, such discoveries should lead to theory building and be subjected to replication, other tests, or both.

(3) An important form of principled discovery is what Julnes (1995) calls the "context-confirmatory approach." Under this approach, an empirical discovery that suggests a mechanism (such as the discovery of differential effects across subgroups on a key outcome) is used to generate a distinct prediction that should be true if the newly induced mechanism is operating (such as the pattern of differences in some other outcomes). (4) It is even possible to obtain evidence of differential effects, without certainty about their origin, by testing for variance shifts that result from the program. Techniques such as those described by Bryk and Raudenbush (1988) can be applied to assess whether treatment groups differ in variability in such a way that would indicate that some unknown interaction exists. For example, if the variability among those assigned to workfare is greater than among those assigned to traditional welfare, this could indicate that workfare is (relatively) helpful to some and harmful to others. Such knowledge (a) could lead to cautions about proposed policy changes and (b) should initiate an exploration to identify what differentiates

those who are helped from those who are hurt. In short, emergent realist evaluators have a considerable array of methods available with which to interrogate the data, which is particularly important when pre-existing theories are not sufficient to guide the search for mechanisms and for the contextual determinants of program outcomes.

"Okay," says your colleague. "I like competitive elaboration and principled discovery as two general strategies. But you mentioned a lot of different ways you could do each of them. How do we decide which specific method to use?"

The concepts of competitive elaboration and principled discovery themselves do not lead magically to method choices. Different methods can be used to carry out competitive elaboration or principled discovery, and the evaluator needs to make an informed choice of methods for the particular evaluation context. With respect to the question of whether to adopt the methods of competitive elaboration or those of principled discovery, the state of existing knowledge will be the primary determinant. The less is known about possible mechanisms, the more likely the evaluator will need to employ the more exploratory techniques of principled discovery, rather than the more verification-oriented techniques of competitive elaboration. But, as suggested by the context-confirmatory approach (Julnes, 1995), the ERE evaluator will probably use both, sometimes in an overlapping fashion and sometimes iterating between the two.

"Let me try this out," interjects your colleague. "Let's say you're evaluating a boot camp program for criminal offenders. You start with a more exploratory analysis, like stuff Tukey wrote about, right? Let's say you find that, compared to the traditional criminal justice system, the boot camp program reduces recidivism for offenders with minor criminal records but not for offenders with more severe records. From that finding, you generate the hypothesis that the mechanism underlying the program is 'labeling': The boot camp keeps minor offenders from getting labeled, by themselves and by others, as criminals." You start to respond, but your colleague continues: "And so from this potential mechanism you develop another hypothesis, such as that, controlling for offense, the program will be more effective for younger than for older offenders because the younger ones will be less likely to have strong labels as criminals." Exactly, you reply, except that the "competitive" part of competitive elaboration kicks in. You also need to identify any alternative mechanisms—whether drawn from the literature, program staff, or clients—such as whether the effects you've mentioned might be caused by motivation or by increased work skills instead of by labeling. And then you try to find predictions that will tell these apart. For example, if it's labeling, the difference between younger and older offenders presumably should be the same at all sites. But if it's work skills, the age difference is likely to depend in predictable ways on the specific activities carried out at each site to teach work skills. After you and your colleague congratulate each other for being able to talk the same language, you decide that you had better clarify the typically iterative relationship between principled discovery and competitive elaboration.

If you start without a strong theory about possible mechanisms, you begin with principled discovery and move on to competitive elaboration as much as possible. On the other hand, if you can identify the possible mechanisms in advance, you start with competitive elaboration and work to collect observations that will help indicate what mechanism is in operation. But you can still do the more exploratory sort of work labeled principled discovery. This may lead to a refined theory of the mechanism (for example, if you find that the relationships predicted by the mechanism hold in some conditions but not in others) or to exploring a possible mechanism you had not identified in advance.

Your colleague jumps in: "Don't I remember seeing something on EvalTalk, or maybe in a review somewhere, that realists don't believe in control or comparison groups? What's this about? Isn't an experimental design going to be helpful sometimes in sorting out competing mechanisms, as well as in just figuring out what the effects of a program are?" I know what you're referring to, you reply. From the ERE perspective, it's a serious flaw in a book that has many other nice attributes.

Pawson and Tilley (1997), working from a scientific realist perspective, have argued against the value of experimental and quasi-experimental control groups. For example, in reviewing one evaluation, they note the study was "a quasi-experimental one, comparing changes between the experimental and control [sites]. However, . . . this cannot add anything instructive, and indeed it does not do so" (Pawson and Tilley, 1997, p. 97). Pawson and Tilley suggest that the "realist experiment" involves creating the conditions that allow one to observe whether a particular mechanism is triggered, and that experimental and quasi-experimental designs are of little value in doing so. On the latter point, ER evaluators disagree. Bhaskar (1978, p. 53), a key figure in critical realism, claimed that there are two functions that the experimental scientist must perform: "First, [s]he must trigger the mechanism under study to ensure that it is active; and, secondly, [s]he must prevent any interference with the operation of the mechanism. These activities could be designated as 'experimental production' and 'experimental control.'" The value of the randomized experiment, as Campbell (1957) suggested, derives from the value of the randomized control group in preventing (or, more precisely, accounting for) the interference of plausible extraneous mechanisms, such as generative mechanisms sparked by other events (history), or emanating from naturally occurring processes within the research participants rather than from the program (maturation). So the ER evaluator sees value in traditional experimental designs, to the extent they aid in principled discovery or competitive elaboration in a given instance.

"Um, where exactly do values fit in here?" your colleague asks, with furrowed brow. Well, you answer, we've kind of ignored values momentarily, but. . .

The sensemaking and values-probing in ER should be linked in an iterative process—a sort of ongoing churning in evaluations and in the policy-making community (Majone, 1988) more broadly. For example, one relatively likely form of this iterative and overlapping focus on values and sensemaking begins with values probes that provide an underpinning for the collection of evidence for sensemaking, which itself will likely entail reinterpretation of evidence and the collection of additional evidence, which is interpreted in light of critical assessment of the values implicit in the evidence, and so on. In addition to feeding into the design and interpretation of the evaluation, findings about values should be communicated to the multiple audiences of the evaluation. While clarity about values conflicts will not lead magically to consensus, it should generally improve the quality of debate and deliberation. To accomplish this interlinking of sensemaking and values-probing, specific approaches or methods for values-probing are required (in addition to the methods for principled discovery and competitive elaboration, which aid sensemaking about program effects and underlying mechanisms). ERE includes three general methodological approaches for values-probing, the purpose of which is to understand the consensus and conflict around values issues among the various groups that have a role in the pluralist, democratic policy processes (Henry, 1996).

The first method involves using sample surveys to better understand the magnitude of concerns about social problems, the perceived need for social or governmental intervention (or for changing an existing intervention), the acceptability of different types of interventions, and what respondents value among the different outcomes an intervention might achieve. For example, in an evaluation of a preschool program for four-year-olds, one might first identify key stakeholder groups, such as teachers, parents, and program administrative staff. In addition, ERE calls for including "the public," which can be represented by a sample of residents in the area served by the program. Each of these groups can be surveyed with two sorts of questions. The first would ask about the extent to which respondents would consider the program a success if it achieved each of a number of different outcomes. Responses to these questions create a *values map,* allowing us to specify whose values are served by particular outcome patterns. A second set of questions can locate the program itself, apart from its observed outcomes, in a values context. For the preschool program, values related to the nature of services and service delivery can be as important as the lists of desired outcomes. For example, one key issue is whether the target population should include only children from "disadvantaged" households (an equity concern) or, alternatively, whether universal access should be provided to this developmental program without targeting specific groups (an equality concern). Similar choices are at the heart of many values issues in American society (Yankelovich, 1994). Other value issues are also of interest, such as parental choice in selecting a preschool program for their child, and the decision about what type of organization should be allowed to provide the services (public, private, or not-for-profit). Survey data on public and stakeholder group views on such questions help in clarifying whose values the intervention represents.

A second approach to values-probing involves the use of any of a number of qualitative methods. Focus groups and intensive interviews can be used to assess the value structure of various stakeholder groups, including the public. Ethnographic observation might also be used to gauge the value positions of program staff and clients. As an example of a qualitative approach to values-probing, Caracelli and Greene (1997) describe an evaluation by Greene and her colleagues of a program that included the elimination of tracking in a school district's science program. This intervention was viewed by minority parents as a way of furthering their children's education, and as the right thing to do. Many other parents saw it as a threat to the quality of their children's preparation for college. Qualitative and quantitative methods were used to "represent pluralistic interests, voices, and perspectives better and, through this representation, both to challenge and transform entrenched positions" (Caracelli and Greene, 1997, p. 29).

A third approach to values-probing falls under the category of *critical analysis*. ER evaluators think of this as a broad category, which can involve examining the value bases of a program (1) from a philosophical perspective on equity, equality, freedom, or other core values, as when House (1988, for example) critiqued programs from the perspective of Rawls' theory of justice, (2) from the perspective of a social philosophy, as illustrated by critiques of social programs from the perspective of feminist theory, or (3) based on a particular methodology that includes critical interpretation of values positions, such as critical discourse (White, 1994). The methodology of critical analysis is designed to expose the biases that lurk in the unthinking acceptance of social values: "[Critical analysis] is wary that any consensus will reflect the interests of those with institutional power in a society and probes for ways to challenge the dominant norms in a society" (White, 1994, p. 519). ERE does not require that critical analyses of these sorts be done, but neither does it discourage them. Such analyses can be revealing about the value issues that drive decisions about a program. However, critical analyses are not a substitute for direct investigation of the value positions of key program stakeholders and the public. Nor is it a substitute for sensemaking activities about the program's effects and underlying mechanisms, although it may lead to a critical examination of the information obtained through such activities.

As with sensemaking, the values-probing component of ERE will often be best served by the use of multiple methods. For example, a sample survey approach may give breadth, in the sense of the ability to generalize about the public's and other stakeholder groups' values (and to compare the values of different groups), whereas focus groups may give depth, in terms of being able to probe deeper into such issues as the reasoning behind particular value positions.

At this point, your colleague interjects, "Hey, does that mean that ERE has a stance on mixing qualitative and quantitative designs? You know how Greene and Caracelli (1997) wrote about different stances on mixed methods?" Well, you reply. . . .

ER evaluators take a positive stance toward mixed-method designs. As Greene and Caracelli (1997) point out, some researchers have claimed that different inquiry paradigms are incompatible and cannot be crossed (for example, see Guba and Lincoln, 1989). Others see the relationship between paradigm and method as weak, and argue for a pragmatic approach to mixing methods (for example, Patton, 1988). The ER position is that the historical paradigms associated with quantitative and qualitative inquiry are not inherently necessary, and that we should not be bound by them in making method choices. Emergent realism shares some similarities with the positivist tradition and some with constructivism, but it remains as an alternative to either. (See Chapter Two of this volume for more detail). According to ERE, the primary considerations that evaluators should use in choosing methods are the ability of the method, in the context of that particular evaluation and its constraints, to (1) further competitive elaboration or principled discovery, as appropriate, (2) clarify the values structure surrounding the program, and (3) address the desired levels of molecularity-molarity. ER evaluators recognize that all of our methods are constructed sensemaking techniques, and all are fallible. In this light, these objectives will often best be served by a combination of quantitative and qualitative methods.

Moreover, when quantitative methods are used, they need to remain flexible for changing questions and for discovery (Mark, Feller, and Button, 1997). Smith (1992; 1997) has similarly advocated flexibility in allowing questions to emerge, although the ERE focus is primarily on the emergence of understanding about mechanism. One strategy that maximizes flexibility is to plan evaluations as a set of smaller, interrelated and sequenced studies, rather than a single large study with a single design (Cronbach, 1982).

"Makes sense to me—although I may have to think a bit more about the paradigm issue. I take it that realism is being proposed as an alternative paradigm. But I don't want to talk about that—I get a headache if I think about 'paradigms' and philosophy of science for too long. How about something more down to earth, like utilization?" Good idea, you say, we need to talk about utilization at some point.

The dual focus on sensemaking and values-probing in ERE exists in light of the corresponding processes that occur in the policy-setting community. For example, in the area of homelessness, sensemaking is involved in such questions as "What is the magnitude of homelessness and who is affected by it," while values are involved in such questions as "What role does society have in preventing or ameliorating the homelessness that exists?" According to ERE, utilization occurs when the sensemaking and values-probing activities of evaluation influence the sensemaking and valuing of the policy-setting community. This can occur at any stage of the policy process (see Chapter Five of this volume).

As suggested in the earlier discussion of evaluation purpose, ERE views explanation—the identification of underlying mechanisms and the conditions under which they are triggered—as an important route to utilization. But it is not the only underlying mechanism for utilization. For example, an evaluation using a randomized experimental design might show that a program has no net effect, but it might provide no information as to why the program did not work. Nevertheless, the results could be used to inform members of the policy community about the existing program and stimulate discourse about changing the program.

Whether or not it is based on explanatory mechanisms, utilization requires generalizing. Inferences are drawn from the concrete observations of an evaluation to other instances where the results will be applied: to the future, certainly, and typically to other settings, to different clients, to variants on the program. Mark (1986) suggested there were three principles that underlie such attempts to generalize (compare to Cook, 1993). The first is the "similarity principle," which involves generalizing to similar instances. This principle is illustrated by Cook and Campbell's (1979) "modal instance" approach to external validity and Cronbach's (1982) recommendation to analyze subsets of the data that correspond most closely to the cases to which one wishes to generalize. Such analyses, along with careful consideration of the similarity between the context of evaluation and that of the desired generalization, can suggest how reasonable it is to generalize in the absence of a sound explanation. A second approach involves the "robustness principle," which involves generalizing based on the finding that the program has had similar effects across diverse contexts (Mark, 1986). The robustness principle underlies Cook and Campbell's (1979) call for "deliberate sampling for heterogeneity" and Cronbach's (1982) similar call for an "extreme groups design" as a way to increase external validity. Emergent realist evaluations will typically assess how robust a program's effect is by testing for interactions with a range of contextual and client variables in the course of competitive elaboration and principled discovery. The third principle that underlies attempts to generalize, according to Mark (1986), is "explanation," which of course is the primary focus of most ERE sensemaking efforts.

You then mention that other specific strategies, such as linking an ERE evaluation with an ongoing monitoring system, such as an MIS, may be useful for making and testing generalizations (Mark, 1995), but that these ideas are tangential to your current focus. "When," your colleague grins, "have we ever let the fact that something is tangential stop us?" It might be a good idea to cut our tangents short, you suggest, at least until after we have done a preliminary project budget. Meanwhile, back to utilization.

One aspect that influences utilization, and is often inadequately discussed in the evaluation literature, involves how to communicate our evaluation results. While a variety of approaches can used in briefings and written reports (for example, see Hendricks, 1994; Patton, 1997), the ER evaluator is especially concerned about communicating the findings to various potential users, including the public. Informing the public necessarily requires concerns for obtaining the information through the existing media channels and working with journalists (Henry, 1996). Graphical displays may be particularly useful (Henry, 1997). For example, for a project evaluating school quality, Henry and others (1996) developed easily interpreted graphical displays, using one to five stars to compare a school with similar schools on each of a set of performance dimensions, and up or down arrows to show the one-year trend in performance.

In addition, it may be useful to attempt to find ways to *socially signify* some results, that is, to describe the magnitude of the impacts in terms that have meaning for the audience. For measures such as recidivism or high school graduation rates, this may not be necessary, because the measure is already in a familiar and commonly understood metric. But the public and other stakeholder groups are often unfamiliar with the meaning of the measures used in evaluations. In such cases, research that translates the measure into more familiar terms may be helpful. For example, in an evaluation of an intervention designed to reduce the time required to hire federal employees, Mark, Feller, and Button (1997) surveyed managers about how much more quickly people would have to be hired to make a real difference in their work units. Sechrest and Yeaton (1981) have made interesting suggestions about how to socially signify results, but it remains an area ripe for future work.

"You know," your colleague says with a big smile on her face, "we could keep on talking about stuff all day, but I think I'm sold. From what I've heard, I like this emergent realist approach. It seems to capture in a coherent way a lot of best practice in evaluation and to add some important features. Let's do this proposal and try to do it from an ERE perspective." You gladly agree, and spend the next weeks stealing time to work on the pre-proposal (the granting agency has solicited short pre-proposals and will solicit complete proposals from a subset of those who submitted pre-proposals). After a couple of revisions, it looks something like this:

Evaluation Plan for the Georgia Pre-Kindergarten Program

Pre-proposal: draft #3

Georgia's Pre-Kindergarten (Pre-K) program is a full-day, developmental preschool program offered to all four-year-olds in the state. Funded by the Georgia Lottery, the program enrolled approximately 62,000 (about 60 percent) of the four-year-olds in the state in the 1996–1997 school year. Explicitly stated program objectives range from improving the educational and social outcomes of the children and their families to increasing human capital and lowering crime rates. The program also appears to have several more implicit objectives, such as reducing the gap between more and less advantaged children, fostering elementary school reform in the state, and engaging parents in actively making educational decisions for their children.

The purpose of this evaluation is five-fold: (1) to understand the extent to which these valued outcomes are obtained by the program participants, their families, and the state; (2) to distinguish which of the plausible program-related mechanisms is most likely to have triggered the attained outcomes; (3) to determine the specific services that trigger the mechanisms for specific groups of children; (4) to examine the extent to which other influences in the children's social worlds, such as parental activities and educational experiences in the K–12 environment, moderate and mediate the attainment of these outcomes; and (5) to probe the consensus or conflict in the public and various stakeholder groups about the values related to the program.

One focus of the evaluation will be on the characteristics of pre-K services delivered, including the type and integrity of the curriculum; teachers' philosophies and practices related to child-centered instruction; quality of the facilities, resources, and instructional program; and organizational factors. These program characteristics are viewed as potential triggers that may initiate specific mechanisms which further a child's development. By relating actual services and specific attributes of services delivery to the attainment of socially desired outcomes by children from a variety of social backgrounds, the evaluation can provide information useful for many groups: for parents to use in choosing a pre-K site and in working with their children and pre-K staff; for program personnel in improving the delivery of services; for program administrators and policy-makers in making systemic changes in the program; and for the public as an informational base in the ongoing policy deliberations concerning the program.

The summary of the evaluation design presented in the next four sections should convey the scope of the proposed research; however, more detailed description of procedures and project management are left for the full proposal. We first describe the values-probing that will provide a mapping of the various outcomes that different groups, including the public, hold as most important for the program. Following that is a brief discussion of the mechanisms that may be stimulated by preschool programs and may underlie the valued outcomes attained by such programs. In the third section, we overview the proposed methods for assessing the program's effects and the causal packages that may lead to specific outcomes. Finally, plans are presented for disseminating the information gained from the evaluation to a variety of groups who may have use for the information.

Methods for Values-Probing. Much is expected of preschool programs in the United States and, more specifically, of Georgia's pre-K program. The importance of preschool programs has been highlighted by scholars of American political opinions and values, who have noted that programs such as Head Start and, by extension, Georgia's pre-K program, provide a mechanism for reconciling the core values of freedom and equality (Yankelovich, 1994). That is, the public holds in general high regard those programs that offer the prospect of creating a level playing field for all.

In the case of the Georgia pre-K program, legislative history and public debate, as well as prior research on related programs, make it possible to develop a reasonably comprehensive list of the possible outcomes of interest. Valued outcomes for the pre-K program range from those involving the participating children, such as improving their cognitive ability and social outcomes, to those involving families, such as improving family circumstances and parental interactions with children, to broader societal benefits, such as lower crime rates and higher rates of educational attainment. In addition, while most potential outcomes derive from and are consistent with stated program objectives, some potential outcomes are not objectives of the program but nevertheless may be highly valued by some group. For example, by providing free day care, the program may allow families to reallocate some funds to other purposes. While not a goal of the program, this may be a highly valued outcome for some stakeholders.

There are several reasons to assess which values are held by which stakeholders. First, the study of values will inform the design of the evaluation, such as the selection of outcomes and mechanisms to be examined. An evaluation should address the question of the effectiveness of a program in terms that reflect the values of those concerned with the program, including the public, upon whom all governmentally provided programs depend for support (Kingdon, 1995). In this, as in most evaluations, resource constraints will presumably preclude evaluating the program's effects on *all* possible outcomes. Instead, because parents, families, program staff, program administrators and policy-makers, and the public all have a stake in the program, it is important to include their most highly valued outcomes. Second, findings about values will be useful in organizing reports about program effects. By knowing the value stances of each group, their perspectives can be better represented in interpretations of the findings. And third, results of the values-probing component of the evaluation will be communicated to the public and to various stakeholder groups, as described in the later section on reporting. Heightened awareness of the value stances of the various groups should enhance the quality of the discussion and debate about the use of other evaluation results.

Although in most past evaluations, any efforts to reflect stakeholders' and the public's values have been informal, two methods are proposed to systematically probe values in this evaluation. First, it is important to establish the outcome preferences of the public and various groups of stakeholders, that is, the pattern of program outcomes which they would consider a success. To obtain systematic information on the outcomes valued by parents, teachers, program administrators, and the public, we propose to conduct sample surveys with each of the four groups. Items will be developed to reflect various possible valued outcomes. These items will stem from a review of enabling legislation, prior public discussion of the program, the research literature, and from consultation with program experts and members of each group to be surveyed. The items will then be included in a self-administered questionnaire for the program administrators and in telephone interviews of the three other groups. For each group, the values will be ranked and analyzed for significant differences. In addition, the results will be compared across groups, and the underlying structure of the responses of the four groups will be analyzed using multiple group structural equation models.

The results of the surveys will subsequently be used to formulate scenarios that highlight trade-offs among highly valued outcomes. These will then be discussed in eight focus groups, with two groups drawn from members of each of the four stakeholder groups. The results will add depth to the survey results and provide information about trade-offs that might result from emphasizing one component of the program at the expense of others.

Potential Underlying Mechanisms. While some past studies show short-term effects of preschool programs on the cognitive ability of participating children, long-term social effects, such as decreased delinquency, higher high school graduation rates, and reduced assignments to special education and remedial education programs, appear to be more common than long-term cognitive gains (Barnett, 1995; Consortium for Longitudinal Studies, 1983; McKey, 1985). Research to date on preschool programs has led to the formulation of several general, alternative mechanisms that may lead to such positive social outcomes (Entwisle, 1995). (1) Preschool may cause short-term but significant cognitive gains, which in turn lead to better placements, such as fewer assignments to special education, remedial education classes, and programs for learning disabled students. By avoiding negative tracking that would otherwise occur (Alexander and Entwisle, 1996), the preschool children do better. (2) Preschool participation may increase the educational expectations of those in the child's social world (parents and teachers), thereby increasing the social resources available to the child and thus increasing the child's attainment. (3) Preschool may effectively promote the development of social skills and behaviors that influence the child's readiness for school as perceived by kindergarten and first-grade teachers. These social skills result in higher placements, higher expectations, and better social outcomes for the children. (4) In a slightly different vein, the preschool experience may be viewed as a part of a continuing educational process, where the gains from one point in the process are mediated by later processes. According to this mechanism, the gains from high-quality, developmentally appropriate instructional programs will be enhanced and maintained by complementary kindergarten programs, but dampened by kindergarten programs that do not have those attributes (Marcon, 1992, 1994; also see Lee and Loeb, 1995).

If one or more of these mechanisms is triggered by the pre-K program, the trigger is presumably some attribute(s) of the pre-K program as it is carried out. Consistent with this belief is evidence that the quality of preschool programs has implications for the cognitive as well as social development of the children, presumably by influencing the extent to which any of the long-term mechanisms are set into place (Marcon, 1994; Carnegie Task Force, 1994). Knowing which attributes of pre-K practice trigger which mechanisms could lead to the design of more effective pre-K programs and could inform parental choice about which pre-K site to attend. Therefore, we propose to examine the potential mechanisms for cognitive gains, enhanced social skills, and increased parental expectations and improved educational resources in the home. This will involve (1) locating or developing, and then applying, a battery of measures of program quality at selected sites and (2) using the methods described in the next section to assess the extent to which any of the mechanisms (see 1–4 in the preceding discussion) appear to be operating. Note, however, that the enumeration of causal mechanisms and therefore the eventual measurement of the indicators of their operation may change, depending on what outcomes are found to be highly valued in the values-probing component of the evaluation.

Methods for Sensemaking. To better understand which of these mechanisms, if any, works for which groups of children and their families, we plan to use several methods for a strategy of competitive elaboration. Competitive elaboration is based on the notion that each of the mechanisms has different implications, which can be thought of as indicators or markers that provide evidence about whether the mechanism is working. For example, one mechanism may involve a particular mediator, that is, an intermediate change that should occur in the middle of the causal sequence between program activities and outcomes. For instance, one mechanism (see item 3, described earlier) indicates that kindergarten and first-grade teachers' ratings of children's school readiness will mediate the effects of quality pre-K on longer-term outcomes. A mechanism can also indicate a particular pattern of moderation, whereby the effects are larger for some types of children and families than others. For instance, one mechanism (see item 1 in preceding discussion), which involves reducing negative tracking, should result in stronger effects for children with lower cognitive skills at entry to pre-K (who are thus initially more at risk for negative tracking). Each of the mechanisms points to specific predictions of moderators, mediators, outcome measures, and sequences of change. In short, competitive elaboration involves assessing the extent to which the particular pattern of predictions associated with each mechanism actually occurs.

Among those areas to be measured in carrying out this process are (1) pre-K program quality; (2) social and behavioral skills of the children; (3) cognitive skills of the children; (4) readiness for schooling; (5) expectations for the child's educational attainment; (6) educational resources in the home, including parent interactions and educational materials; (7) program quality in school, beginning with kindergarten; and (8) outcome measures, such as attendance, promotions or retentions, and program assignments. We will also measure certain variables that are subject to state regulation or that may facilitate parental choice of programs for their children and might be related to program outcomes (such as teachers' credentials and type of instructional curriculum). In addition to these measures, certain control variables, such as the socioeconomic status of the families, will be collected because of the pervasive evidence of the influence of family background on educational achievement and attainment.

Consistent with the request for proposals, we propose to follow a cohort of pre-K participants and their families for five years. For most of the students, we anticipate that the four-year-olds in the cohort will progress to the third grade, the point at which statewide tests of academic skills are available. A brief schedule of surveys, classified by respondent group, and a list of observations that are proposed for systematic data collection are shown in Table 1.1.

Although the request for proposal specifies that a cohort of pre-K participants and their families be followed, it does not specify that a control group of non–pre-K students and families be included in the design. Apart from the issue of budget, the construction of a non–pre-K control group is complicated by the fact that the program is universally available to all preschoolers and their families in the state. Thus, the proposed evaluation emphasizes comparisons within the program, across variations in program curriculum, implementation quality, and type of site (as well as the way such factors differentially affect different types of children). Nevertheless, we propose two strategies for assessing, to the extent possible, the overall effect of the program. First, a small cohort control group will be constructed based on the reports of older siblings of participating children. Second, time series data will be collected on academic outcomes in the early grades, at those school districts at which the records are available, to look for overall improvements related to the level of participation in the pre-K program.

In addition to examining the relationships predicted by those mechanisms identified a priori, we will adopt an additional analytical strategy of principled discovery. Prior research does not provide an adequate base for predictions about how the mechanisms described previously may operate differently for different groups of students. The effect of the program on different subgroups is, of course, an important question. For example, at least some stakeholders would respond differently if the program had a large positive effect on children from disadvantaged households and little effect on children from advantaged households, relative to how they would react if the program had a large positive effect on the advantaged and no effect on the disadvantaged. And differential effects seem plausible. For example, pre-K may increase parental expectations more for students from disadvantaged households than for other children, which could in turn result in more beneficial long-term effects. Methods such as structural equation models can be used to test these differences. Findings about such differences would lead to other sets of predictions, for example, about the change that should occur in parental behaviors across different subgroups of parents. Testing these "second-generation" predictions helps to demonstrate that the original findings (in this example, about parental expectations) were not spurious; hence the term *principled discovery*.

Reporting. We propose several deliverables. First, annual reports will summarize project activities and findings to date, with detailed documentation of the methods and findings. Actual data, without any identifying information, will be made available to the evaluation sponsors and, upon request, to others. A four-page (maximum) brief will also be prepared for policy audiences. During the second year of the project, a parent's guide for choosing a pre-K site for their child will be developed; this will subsequently be updated, as needed,

Table 1.1 Pre-Kindergarten Evaluation: A Pre-Proposal Data Collection Plan

	Year of Study				
Type of Data Collection	*1* *Pre-K*	*2* *Kindergarten*	*3* *1st Grade*	*4* *2nd Grade*	*5* *3rd Grade*
Classroom Observation	❖	❖			
Program Director/Principal Interviews	❖				
Principal Questionnaire	❖	❖			
Teacher Personal Interviews	❖	❖			
Teacher Telephone Survey		❖	❖	❖	❖
Teacher Administered Tests	❖	❖			
Standardized Tests	❖		❖		❖
Student Progress/Attendance	❖	❖	❖	❖	❖
Parental Telephone Interviews	❖	❖			❖

based on subsequent research findings. In addition, a parent's guide to interacting with the pre-K staff and enhancing their child's development will be developed, using the evaluation findings and other research. Finally, the media will be provided with press releases and reports to convey the findings to the public. It is important for the public and parents to have the best available information to know both the extent to which the program is fulfilling their expectations and the steps taken by the program administrators to enhance the prospect of meeting public expectations. Therefore, the evaluators will work closely with the program administrators in sharing the information with the public.

On Generalizing. For the findings of this evaluation to be useful, they should support generalizations that apply beyond the observed sample to other preschoolers, parents, and preschool sites in Georgia. In addition, Georgia is the first state in the nation to offer a universal, developmental program for four-year-olds, and the results of the proposed evaluation may accordingly be of considerable interest outside as well within the state. In this section, we consider how the results obtained in the proposed evaluation may be useful beyond the specific program sites that are included in the evaluation.

First, we plan to select a probability sample of 200 to 220 of the sites that are currently providing pre-K services to four-year-olds. The sample will be stratified by (1) region of the state; (2) type of organization offering the services (private or local school system); and (3) type of curriculum offered at the site. While the stratification will be complex, it offers several advantages. The sampling strategy will enhance the following factors: the generalizability of the findings within the state; the ability to test for the moderating effects of the stratifying variables; the power of the statistical tests (by way of the lower standard errors, given the sample size); and the credibility of the evaluation. However, while it facilitates generalization within the state of Georgia, the sampling strategy will not in a formal sampling sense allow extrapolating results beyond the state borders.

Extrapolating the results beyond the scope of the sampling frame (in this case, to other states) has noteworthy historical precedent in the area of preschool programs. In particular, many unconstrained generalizations have been based on the results of the Perry Preschool Project in Ypsilanti, Michigan (see Wilson, 1994, for a brief critique). In a very real way, the proposed evaluation contains the basis for generalization as well as for the specification of limits on generalization. Analyses will be provided for different types of children and families (for example, economically advantaged and disadvantaged), settings (such as urban and rural), and curricula. Other states considering a similar pre-K program can see whether the program was successful in those cases similar to the cases that predominate in their populations. In addition, attempts to generalize should be enhanced by the proposed evaluation strategy of linking site-level program activity with the mechanisms that may result in desired outcomes. By improving knowledge on *why* pre-K works as it does, evaluation results should contribute to decisions by other states about whether to implement a similar program, as well as to decisions within Georgia on how to improve the program.

At the end of an e-mailed set of comments and revisions to the draft proposal, your colleague writes, "I think we're on to something with this emergent realist evaluation. Where does it go from here?" You e-mail back that her question has led you to think a bit about three points related to the role of ERE in the profession of evaluation.

First, according to ERE, the theory and practice of evaluation is in a state of ongoing development (or emergence). Consequently, ERE will appear somewhat different in another decade and will make somewhat different recommendations for practice, in light of forthcoming developments in theory, method, and practice-based lessons. Second, while ER evaluators may sometimes seem evangelical, attempting to "spread the faith" *(as you did with your colleague),* they do not believe in a single, universal religion of evaluation. To the contrary, ER evaluators are happy to see other evaluators following different approaches (such as Patton-style evaluation, which overlaps at least some of the time with organizational development, or Scriven-like assessments of merit and worth without the attention to underlying mechanisms), even though, from the lens of ERE, these types of evaluations have limited usefulness. Still, ERE advocates believe that programs can fruitfully be examined at different levels and at different stages of development, and they see these other approaches as providing aspects of a comprehensive ER evaluation. In this sense, the ER approach to knowledge and values provides a framework for considering the contribution of various approaches to evaluation, and of individual evaluations, in terms of the limitations of the sensemaking technologies employed and the values considered. Use of ERE for such a framework should contribute to that "disputatious community of scholars" (Campbell, 1984) who can talk to each other and debate matters of substance without allowing approach-based differences in terminology to segment conversations into a Tower of Babel. While a healthy profession of evaluation need not be monolithic, forums and language for discussions are vital. And third, as an ER evaluator, you hope that training in ER-based methods, such as methods for values-probing and principled discovery, will become more common.

You sign off your e-mail, smiling to yourself as an old Temptations song plays on the radio. You feel eager to read more about ERE and to apply it to your future evaluation work.

References

Alexander, K., and Entwisle, D. "Educational Tracking During the Early Years: First-Grade Placements and Middle-School Constraints. "In A. Kerckhoff (ed.), *Generating Social Stratification: Toward a New Research Agenda.* Boulder, Colo. Westview Press, 1996.

Barnett, W. "Long-Term Effects of Early Childhood Programs on Cognitive and School Outcomes." *The Future of Children,* 1995, 5 (3), 25–49.

Bhaskar, R. A. *A Realist Theory of Science.* Atlantic Highlands, N.J.: Humanities Press, 1978.

Borkovec, T. D., and Miranda, J. "Between-Group Psychotherapy Outcome Research and

Basic Science." *Psychotherapy and Rehabilitation Research Bulletin,* 1996, *5,* 14–20.

Bryk, A. S., and Raudenbush, S. W. "On Heterogeneity of Variance in Experimental Studies: A Challenge to Conventional Interpretation." *Psychological Bulletin,* 1988, *104,* 396–404.

Bryk, A. S., and Raudenbush, S. W. *Hierarchical Linear Models: Applications and Data Analysis Methods.* Newbury Park, Calif.: Sage, 1992.

Campbell, D. T. "Factors Relevant to the Validity of Experiments in Social Settings." *Psychological Bulletin,* 1957, *54,* 456–453.

Campbell, D. T. "Pattern Matching as an Essential in Distal Knowing." In K. R. Hammond (ed.), *The Psychology of Egon Brunswik.* New York: Holt, Rinehart and Winston, 1966.

Campbell, D. T. "Qualitative Knowing in Action Research." Kurt Lewin Address; Annual meeting of the American Psychological Association, New Orleans, La., 1974.

Campbell, D. T. "Can We Be Scientific in Applied Social Science?" In R. F. Connor, D.`G. Altman, and C. Jackson (eds.), *Evaluation Studies Review Annual,* Vol. 9. Newbury Park, Calif.: Sage, 1984.

Caracelli, V. J., and Greene, J. C. "Crafting Mixed-Method Evaluation Designs." In J. C. Greene and D. J. Caracelli (eds.), *Advances in Mixed-Method Evaluation: The Challenges and Benefits of Integrating Diverse Paradigms.* New Directions for Evaluation, no. 74. San Francisco: Jossey-Bass, 1997.

Carey, T. S., and others. "The Outcomes and Costs of Care for Acute Back Pain Among Patients Seen by Primary Care Practitioners, Chiropractors, and Orthopedic Surgeons: The North Carolina Back Pain Project." *New England Journal of Medicine,* 1995, *333* (14), 913–917.

Carnegie Task Force on Meeting the Needs of Young Children. *Starting Points: Meeting the Needs of Our Youngest Children.* 1994.

Consortium for Longitudinal Studies (ed.). *As the Twig is Bent . . . : Lasting Effects of Preschool Programs.* Hillsdale, N.J.: Erlbaum, 1983.

Cook, T. D. "Postpositivist Critical Multiplism." In R. L. Shotland and M. M. Mark (eds.), *Social Science and Social Policy.* Beverly Hills, Calif.: Sage, 1985.

Cook, T. D. "A Quasi-Sampling Theory of the Generalization of Causal Relationships." In L. B. Sechrest and A. G. Scott (eds.), *Understanding Causes and Generalizing About Them.* New Directions for Program Evaluation, no. 57, 1993.

Cook, T. D., and others. *Meta-Analysis for Explanation: A Casebook.* New York: Russell Sage Foundation, 1992.

Cook, T. D., and Campbell, D. T. *Quasi-Experimentation: Design and Analysis Issues for Field Settings.* Chicago: Rand McNally, 1979.

Cronbach, L. J. "Beyond the Two Disciplines of Scientific Psychology." *American Psychologist,* 1975, *30,* 116–127.

Cronbach, L. J. *Designing Evaluations of Educational and Social Programs.* San Francisco: Jossey-Bass, 1982.

Entwisle, D. "The Role of Schools in Sustaining Early Childhood Program Benefits." *The Future of Children: Long-Term Outcomes of Early Childhood Programs,* 1995, *5* (3), 133–144.

Gamoron, A. "Educational Stratification and Individual Careers." In A. Kerckhoff (ed.), *Generating Social Stratification: Toward a New Research Agenda.* Boulder, Colo.: Westview Press, 1996.

Greene, J. C., and Caracelli, V. J. "Defining and Describing the Paradigm Issue in Mixed-Method Evaluation." In J. C. Greene and D. J. Caracelli (eds.) *Advances in Mixed-Method Evaluation: The Challenges and Benefits of Integrating Diverse Paradigms.* New Directions for Evaluation, no. 74. San Francisco: Jossey-Bass, 1997.

Guba, E .G., and Lincoln, Y. S. *Fourth-Generation Evaluation.* Newbury Park, Calif.: Sage, 1989.

Hanushek, 1997

Hendricks, M. "Making a Splash: Reporting Evaluation Results Effectively." In J. S. Wholey, H. P. Hatry, K. E. Newcomer (eds.) *Handbook of Practical Program Evaluation.* San Fransisco, Jossey-Bass, 1994.

Henry, G. T. *Graphing Data: Techniques for Display and Analysis.* Thousand Oaks, Calif.: Sage, 1995.

Henry, G. T. "Community-Based Accountability: A Theory of Accountability and School Improvement." *Phi Delta Kappan,* 1996, *78* (1), 85–90.

Henry, G. T. *Creating Effective Graphs: Solutions for a Variety of Evaluation Data.* New Directions for Evaluation, no. 73. San Francisco: Jossey-Bass, 1997.

Henry, G., and Bugler, D. *Evaluation of the Georgia HOPE Scholarship Program: Impact on Students Attending Public Colleges and Universities.* Atlanta, Ga.: Council for School Performance Report, 1997.

Henry, G. T. and others. *School Performance Reports.* Atlanta, Ga.: Council for School Performance. 1996.

House, E. R. *Jesse Jackson and the Politics of Charisma: The Rise and Fall of the PUSH/Excel Program.* Boulder, Colo.: Westview, 1988.

House, E. R. "Realism in Research." *Educational Researcher,* 1991, *20,* 2–9.

Jones, J., Dolan, K., and Henry, G. *Two Miles Down a Ten-Mile Road: Instructional Technology and the Impact of Lottery Funding in Georgia.* Council for School Performance, 1996.

Julnes, G. "Context-Confirmatory Methods for Supporting Disciplined Induction in Post-Positivist Inquiry." Paper presented at the annual meeting of the American Evaluation Association, Vancouver, British Columbia, November 2, 1995.

Kingdon, J. *Agendas, Alternatives, and Public Policies.* (2nd ed.) HarperCollins, 1995.

Lee, V., and Leob, S. "Where Do Head Start Attendees End Up? One Reason Why Preschool Effects Fade Out." *Educational Evaluation and Policy Analysis,* 1995, *17* (1), 62–82.

Majone, G. *Evidence, Argument, and Persuasion in the Policy Process.* New Haven, Conn.: Yale University Press, 1988.

Marcon, R. "Differential Effects of Three Preschool Models on Inner-City Four-Year-Olds." *Early Childhood Research Quarterly,* 1992, *7,* 517–530.

Marcon, R. *Early Learning and Early Identification Follow-Up Study: Transition from the Early to the Later Childhood Grades.* Washington, D.C., 1994, 1–22. (ED 263984)

Mark, M. M. "Validity Typologies and the Logic and Practice of Quasi-Experimentation." In W.M.K. Trochim (ed.), *Advances in Quasi-Experimental Design and Analysis.* New Directions for Program Evaluation, no. 31. San Francisco: Jossey-Bass, 1986.

Mark, M. M. "From Program Theory to Tests of Program Theory." In L. Bickman (ed.), *Advances in Program Theory.* New Directions for Program Evaluation, no. 47. San Francisco: Jossey Bass, 1990.

Mark, M. M. "On the Integration of Discovery, Confirmation, and Monitoring in Evaluation." Paper presented at the Trinity Symposium on Public Management Research. San Antonio, Tex., 1995.

Mark, M. M., Feller, I., and Button, S. B. "Integrating Qualitative Methods in a Predominantly Quantitative Evaluation: A Case Study and Some Reflections." In J. C. Greene and D. J. Caracelli (eds.), *Advances in Mixed-Method Evaluation: The Challenges and Benefits of Integrating Diverse Paradigms.* New Directions for Evaluation, no. 74. San Francisco: Jossey-Bass, 1997.

Mark, M. M., Henry, G. T., and Julnes, G. "Evaluation, A Realist Approach: Monitoring, Classification, Causal Analysis, and Values Inquiry." In preparation.

Mark, M. M., Hofmann, D., and Reichardt, C. S. "Testing Theories in Theory-Driven Evaluations: (Tests of) Moderation in All Things." In H.-t. Chen and P. H. Rossi (eds.), *Using Theory to Improve Program and Policy Evaluations.* New York: Greenwood Press, 1992.

Maxwell, J. *Qualitative Research Design: An Interactive Approach.* Thousand Oaks, Calif.: Sage, 1996.

McKey, R. *The Impact of Head Start on Children, Families, and Communities.* Washington, D.C., 1985. (ED 263984)

Mohr, L. B. *Impact Analysis of Program Evaluation.* (2nd ed.) Thousand Oaks, Calif.: Sage, 1995.

Patton, M. Q. "Paradigms and Pragmatism." In D. M. Fetterman (ed.), *Qualitative Approaches to Evaluation in Education: The Silent Scientific Revolution.* New York: Praeger, 1988.

Patton, M. Q. *Utilization-Focused Evaluation: The New Century Text.* Thousand Oaks, Calif.: Sage, 1997.

Pawson, R., and Tilley, N. *Realistic Evaluation.* Thousand Oaks, Calif.: Sage, 1997.

Reichardt, C. S., and Mark, M. M. "Quasi-Experimentation." In L. Bickman and D. J. Rog (eds.), *Handbook of Applied Social Research Methods.* Thousand Oaks, Calif.: Sage, 1998.

Ross, L. and Nisbett, R. E. *The Person and the Situation.* New York: McGraw Hill, 1991.

Ross, H. L., Campbell, D. T., and Glass, G. V. "Determining the Social Effects of Legal Reform: The British 'Breathalyser' Crackdown in 1967." *American Behavioral Scientist,* 1970, *13,* 493–509.

Scriven, M. *The Evaluation Thesaurus.* Thousand Oaks, Calif.: Sage, 1990.

Sechrest, L., and Yeaton, W. E. "Assessing the Effectiveness of Social Programs: Methodological and Conceptual Issues." In S. Ball (ed.), *Assessing and Interpreting Outcomes.* New Directions for Program Evaluation, no. 9. San Francisco: Jossey Bass, 1981.

Shadish, W. R., Cook, T. D., and Leviton, L. C. *Foundations of Program Evaluation: Theories of Practice.* Newbury Park, Calif.: Sage, 1991.

Smith, M. L. "Mixing and Matching: Methods and Models." In J. C. Greene and D. J. Caracelli (eds.), *Advances in Mixed-Method Evaluation: The Challenges and Benefits of Integrating Diverse Paradigms.* New Directions for Evaluation, no. 74. San Francisco: Jossey-Bass, 1997.

Smith, N. L. "Aspects of Investigative Inquiry in Evaluation." In N.L. Smith (ed), *Varieties of Investigate Evaluation.* New Directions for Program Evaluation, no. 50. San Francisco: Jossey Bass, 1992.

Trochim, W.M.K. "Pattern Matching, Construct Validity, and Conceptualization in Program Evaluation." *Evaluation Review,* 1985, *9,* 575–604.

Tukey, J. W. *Exploratory Data Analysis.* Reading, Mass.: Addison-Wesley, 1977.

White, L. "Policy Analysis as Discourse." *Journal of Policy Analysis and Management,* 1994, *12* (3), 322–359.

Wholey, J. S. "Evaluability Assessment: Developing Program Theory." In L. Bickman (ed.), *Using Program Theory in Evaluation.* New Directions in Program Evaluation, no. 33. San Francisco: Jossey-Bass, 1987.

Wilson, J. "Culture, Incentives, and the Underclass." In H. J. Aaron, T. E. Mann, and T. Taylor (eds). *Values and Public Policy.* Washington, D.C.: The Brookings Institution, 1994.

Wright, J. D. "Methodological Issues in Evaluating the National Health Care for the Homeless Program." In D. J. Rog (ed.), New Directions for Program Evaluation, no. 52. San Francisco: Jossey-Bass, 1991.

Yankelovich, D. "How Changes in the Economy are Reshaping American Values." In H. J. Aaron, T. E. Mann, and T. Taylor (eds), *Values and Public Policy.* Washington, D.C.: The Brookings Institution, 1994.

Yin, R. K. *Case Study Research: Design and Methods.* (2nd ed.) Thousand Oaks, Calif.: Sage, 1994.

Realism offers an alternative to the traditional positivist and constructivist paradigms. The principles of this approach are described here, as are its implications for knowledge construction.

Evaluation as Sensemaking: Knowledge Construction in a Realist World

George Julnes, Melvin M. Mark

At its best, evaluation gives warrant to action. For example, evaluation can undergird decisions by policy makers to continue, expand, revise, or curtail programs; by program managers and staff to change program practices; and by potential clients to enter a program or not. These decisions have real consequences— misguided choices can lead to squandered resources and unnecessary human suffering. If evaluation aids in giving warrant to action, it does so in part by helping us reach conclusions about the likely consequences of programs. But on what basis, and by what methods, should evaluation provide warranted conclusions?

The knowledge component of an evaluation theory addresses this question. According to Shadish, Cook, and Leviton (1991), the knowledge component addresses ontology (the nature of the world), epistemology (how we come to know about the world, that is, the justification for knowledge claims), and methodology (the techniques we use to construct our knowledge claims). We will address all three of these issues, though we shall avoid frequent use of terms such as ontology and epistemology.

The knowledge component of evaluation theory is important because it provides the foundation for two key decisions an evaluator must address in planning and carrying out an evaluation. First, which of the forms of knowledge an evaluation might address are most important in a particular evaluation? For example, should the evaluation emphasize estimating program effects, explaining why program effects occurred, measuring the scope of program coverage, assessing fidelity to the treatment plan, or measuring program

New Directions for Evaluation, no. 78, Summer 1998 © Jossey-Bass Publishers costs? Second, what methods and strategies should be used in a particular evaluation? Before addressing these and related questions from an emergent realist perspective, we provide a brief historical review of realism as a response to the two most visible approaches to knowledge construction, approaches that have fueled many of the debates in evaluation.

An Abbreviated Sketch of the Paradigm Wars

Evaluation, as with many disciplines, has been dominated by two opposing views of how we understand our world: a validation paradigm based on logical positivism and its derivations, and an interpretivist paradigm, which has offspring such as radical constructivism. These paradigms have long opposed each other, with each becoming ascendent for a time only to have its inherent flaws lead to the other's resurgence (Sorokin, 1957). Despite the demonstrated inadequacies of each, these two views dominate the debate over the proper foundation for evaluation.

Logical Positivism and its Legacy. For many, the justification for arriving at warranted conclusions in early modern evaluation was provided by the experimental method and a perspective historically associated with logical positivism. Logical positivism, which can be traced back to Comte and the Enlightenment, developed largely as a response to the speculative claims, not amenable to verification, that dominated philosophy in nineteenth-century Europe.

Validation of Causal Relationships. The positivist effort to avoid speculative conclusions evolved through a series of received methodologies. First, following Hume, positivists were staunch empiricists who sought to avoid claims that could not be substantiated by direct experience. This emphasis on experience, however, made claims about causal relationships problematic. Because one never sees "causation" directly, positivists, inspired by Hume, insisted that inferring cause requires observing a constant conjunction between presumed cause and effect (that is, the effect is observed if and only if the cause is observed), as well as observing a contiguity between the cause and the effect, with temporal precedence of the cause.

While positivists' emphasis on empirical data helped reduce uncontrolled speculation in theories of social behavior, the induction of general laws from observed regularities is vulnerable to spurious associations. In positivism's second stage, the "hypothetico-deductive model" was used to derive predictions explicitly from theory that could then be tested for confirmation (Fiegl, 1973). This approach was thought to test theory using deduction rather than induction and thus reduce the risk of capitalizing on chance. However, this validation approach involves a logical error known by such fancy names as "affirming the consequent," "the fallacy of the undistributed middle," or "modus tollens." This error can be stated much more simply: It is possible to be right for the wrong reason. Confirmation of one's predictions does not ensure that one's theory is true—perhaps some other, better theory applies and would make the same predictions.

Recognizing this logical fallacy, Popper (1968) rejected confirmationism of even the hypothetico-deductive variety (with its necessary, if disguised, reliance on induction). Instead, Popper insisted that the advance of scientific knowledge depended on *falsification* of *incorrect* assumptions: By gradually winnowing out incorrect conclusions, we will be left with more adequate conclusions. Although Popper was not a logical positivist, his critique of the problem of induction led to falsificationism being accepted as the received view in the third stage of the validation paradigm. For this third stage, under the influence of Popper and the scientific realism of Reichenbach, logical empiricism replaced logical positivism, but in many ways the goal remained the same. As with their predecessors, logical empiricists hoped to develop laws that "(with the help of descriptions of 'initial and boundary conditions') even all the individual facts and events of the world could (in principle) be derived" (Feigl, 1973, p. 548).

Validation and the Problem of Trivial Theory. The positivist tradition contributed to the development of inquiry methods that support conclusions with observed data. Nonetheless, serious problems result from its strict commitment to validation. In addition to the inadequate attention given to discovery, the validation paradigm is based on a philosophy that assumes the validity of general laws. Modern critics argue that when used with the open systems that characterize social life, as opposed to the closed systems created in experimental laboratories, the validation paradigm becomes vulnerable to the problem of moderated relationships (that is, unknown interactions that limit one's conclusions and one's ability to generalize, and so create difficulties for falsification). Validation, if unable to incorporate moderating contextual factors, would provide overly general conclusions about a reality that is more finely nuanced. For managers or policy-makers who need to make decisions appropriate for specific contexts, the general theory produced by the validation paradigm may, therefore, be trivial.

The Challenge of Radical Constructivism. Aware of the limits of the standard validation approach, many scholars in evaluation and elsewhere in the social sciences were drawn to an alternative framework that was developed from longstanding traditions in anthropology and parts of sociology. In fact, a number of overlapping frameworks emerged, referred to by such labels as constructivism, interpretivism, naturalism, and feminist methodology.

Constructivism and Multiple Realities. There are many forms of constructivism, but common to many, and in stark contrast to the logical empiricists' objective stance, is a belief in subjective idealism. That is, these frameworks deny that there is any reality separate from experience. Instead, individual interpretations are thought to be all that exist. Because differing interpretations are deemed equally valid, these constructivists talk not of reality but of multiple realities (Guba, 1990). Constructivist research tends to focus on participants' perspectives and on the meaning that participants ascribe to experiences(such as participating in a program), rather than on the relationships among variables. Generalization is typically not given priority as a goal; instead, the focus is on particularities and specific contexts (generalization is often thought of as unattainable in these frameworks). Knowledge claims are 'thought to be based not on the empirical tests of the validation paradigm, but on the *hermeneutic circle,* an iterative procedure of interpreting interpretations with no fixed ending or "rule book" (Smith and Heshusius, 1986).

Constructivism and the Problem of Program Impacts. Although constructivism provides needed criticism of the validation tradition, we also believe it is wrong-headed and impractical for evaluators. Radical constructivism denies an observer-independent reality of social processes, and it is inattentive to causality (indeed, constructivists commonly deny the meaningfulness of the concept of causality). This in turn allows inattention to methodological controls, as well as the avoidance of important questions for evaluation, such as, What are the effects of the program? Smith (1994, p. 42) summarizes the problems well: "The stand of the constructivists—that since realities are multiple, truth relative, and accounts equally true or false, the best we as evaluators can do is to produce journalistic narratives—begs the question of rigor and rationality, effectively takes evaluators out of the conversation, and obviates the necessity to do good." Pragmatically, it seems that few contracts will be awarded to the evaluator whose proposals begin, "There is no reality."

Realist Alternative. The two historically dominant paradigms present a stark choice for evaluators. Are we to choose, in Bhaskar's words, between "either a conceptually impoverished and deconceptualizing empiricism, or a hermeneutics drained of causal import and impervious to empirical controls" (1989a, p. 12)? We believe, with Bhaskar and others, that this is an artificial and dispiriting choice, and so we promote an alternative based on the philosophical paradigm known as realism.

Development of Realism. Realism is not a new paradigm. John Locke's seventeenth-century *representational realism* was based on his distinction between sensation and perception. Locke claimed that our senses react to the real world around us, but that these sensations—and thus reality—are not experienced directly. Rather, sensations provide the raw material that our mind organizes into perceptions. One function of Locke's realism was to encourage a critical view of then-current empirical and idealist claims to Truth.

During the twentieth century, variants of Locke's realism have again been proposed to counter the excesses of empiricism and constructivism. *New realism* was developed in 1910 in reaction to the mentalism of German Idealism. *Critical realism,* which followed a decade later (Drake and others, 1920), re-emphasized the skepticism neglected by the new realists. *Scientific realism* (promoted by Reichenbach and W. S. Sellars), on the other hand, developed during the middle of this century as the physical sciences made important advances. Scientific realism was a return to strict empiricism and emphasized the virtual inevitability of scientific progress as scientific accounts would replace flawed, everyday understandings. The difficulty in achieving the promise of scientific realism led to renewed neo-realist efforts to counter the excesses of empiricism: Bhaskar (1975, 1989b), Cook and Campbell (1979), Putnam (1990, 1995), Harre (1986), House, (1991), and Pawson and Tilley (1997). Several of these theories are familiar to many evaluators, but we believe the modern realist position, confounded as it has been with earlier versions of realism, has not yet received the attention it deserves.

Introduction to Modern Realism. Modern realism, or neo-realism, involves elements of both empiricism and constructivism. Table 2.1 presents several of the opposing positions associated with the validation and interpretivist paradigms, along with the realist responses to these artificial choices (see Putnam, 1990). Taking the first row, for example, realism shares with empiricism the belief that there is a real world that exists apart from human constructions (and that humans often benefit by better understanding that world). At the same time, realism shares with constructivism the belief that our experience of the world is not direct, that our perception of reality is mediated by what we bring to the experience, and, thus, that our experience of reality is constructed. This bridging of empiricism and constructivism, is not, however, a pragmatic eclecticism. Rather, realism is an alternative, coherent foundation that succeeds by rejecting the artificial dichotomies in Table 2.1 that distract us from real human sensemaking. The realist view of theory, described later, also integrates empiricist and constructivist insights. Realists view theory as a cognitive support that enables us to see patterns otherwise unavailable to us. In addition to supporting warranted action, the patterns thus perceived by theory-informed inquiry then guide the development of more adequate cognitive supports.

Table 2.1. Traditional Dichotomies and Realist Responses

Validation Paradigm	Interpretivist Paradigm	Neo-Realism
Real world; objectively experienced	Subjective reality; constructed experience	Real world; constructed experience
General laws	Context-specific interpretations	Casual regularities
Reductionism	Holistic complexity	Embedded systems
Mechanical causes	Intentionality	Emergent order
Formal deduction	Open induction	Natural sensemaking
Valid knowledge	Intersubjective consensus	Warranted beliefs and actions

Foundations of Knowledge Construction in Emergent Realist Evaluation

Having highlighted how the basic ideas of realism differ from those of the positivist and interpretativist traditions, we now present four conceptual themes of our version of realism, emergent realism. (1) As a foundation, we emphasize that our position follows in the tradition of *commonsense realism*, a tradition that recognizes both the limitations and the abilities of humans to make sense of their complex social world. (2) We describe the implications of viewing social reality in terms of the contextual dynamics of complex open systems, in which the predictable results desired in controlled experiments become an unrealistic ideal. (3) We contend that the world is organized in terms of different levels, implying that humans can make sense of the social world, for example, with causal factors operating at the molar level of social structures and also at the more molecular level of individual motivations. (4) Emergent realism accepts the emergentist principle (see, for example, Campbell, 1974b), which contends that (a) evolution has produced increasingly complex biological and social processes, and (b) the mechanistic models that underlie most social science theories provide a useful approximation but never capture and convey all of the complexity of interest.

We believe these themes define a position that accepts the real world the later empiricists sought to understand, while it rejects the presumed objectivity that the constructivists appropriately criticized. Further, the framework can account for complex emergent phenomena that do not fit more positivist explanations, without sacrificing the commonsense realism that some constructivists have abandoned.

Commonsense Realism. Emergent realism is a variety of commonsense realism. This means that our commonsense experience of the world is allowed some standing when we develop and evaluate the formal theories that attempt to provide systematic accounts of that experience. Given the nature of reality and the nature of understanding, emergent realists agree with Meehl when he says,

> As to realism, I have never met any scientist who, when doing science, held to a phenomenalist or idealist view; and I cannot force myself to take a nonrealist view seriously even when I work at it. So I begin with the presupposition that the external world is really there, there is a difference between the world and my view of it, and the business of science is to get my view in harmony with the way the world really is to the extent that is possible (1986, p. 322).

Nature of Reality. Two assumptions about reality ground the emergent realist position: (1) Reality exists, and (2) meaningful patterns are present in this reality.

Echoing Meehl, Bhaskar (1989b) cites Bachelard to argue that all social theorists are realists in the sense of believing in an external reality—their very actions betray such a belief. In this regard, realism coincides with positivism but stands in stark contrast to the idealism put forth by some interpretivist evaluation theorists, whose argument for "multiple realities" is based on the assumption that there is no reality other than those created by our awareness. With Meehl and Bhaskar, we cannot comprehend a rationale for doing evaluation if we deny the presupposition that the external world is really there. On the other hand, as we note later, our understanding of this reality is not the straightforward task that earlier positivists had hoped.

The second aspect of commonsense realism involves a belief in the presence of meaningful patterns. This includes a belief about two types of patterns—causal regularities and natural categories. With the empiricists, realists believe that *causal regularities* exist independently of our awareness of them (Bhaskar, 1989b). Gravity did not wait to operate until humans mentally constructed it. Nor have most social forces. On the other hand, consistent with constructivism, complexities do exist in the social domain such that humans' awareness of social processes can impact the processes themselves (Gergen, 1973; Mohr, 1996). For example, if workers become aware that their employer is trying to manipulate their behavior using some influence process, their reaction may be different than if they were unaware of the employer's tactics. Such reactions, however, do not void the claim that causal regularities exist independent of our awareness. Indeed, in this example, the reactive effect of the workers' awareness could be real even if no one had yet recognized its existence.

As for natural categories, realists take seriously the notion of *natural kinds* (Bhaskar, 1989b; Aronson, Harre, and Way, 1995). The commonsense position is simply that there are natural and meaningful groupings of many things in our world. The groupings are meaningful even though the groups can always be analyzed in finer detail to reveal further meaningful differences. Not all useful category schemes involve natural kinds, but we believe that some do. Realist philosophers use examples such as carbon atoms to claim that some categories exist independently of our construction of them. Realist conceptions about natural kinds can be useful in considering a variety of issues in evaluation, such as whether it is meaningful to make statements about the aggregate impact of the program; whether and how one should identify groupings of projects or sites within a program; and whether a program or project is implemented faithfully. A thorough investigation of these applications of emergent realism is forthcoming (Mark, Henry, and Julnes, in preparation).

Nature of Understanding: Naturalized Epistemology. How do we come to know about the world? According to emergent realism, we have evolved to make sense of our world in meaningful ways, but this evolved capacity is limited. We use the term *sensemaking* to describe efforts to construct meaningful order, thus differentiating this process from more positivistic efforts aimed at revealing laws and truth as though seen, in Putnam's (1990) words, with a "God's-Eye View." Sensemaking is part of a naturalized epistemology, where *naturalized* refers to a faith in the natural capacities of human sensemaking and a rejection of overly formal accounts of knowledge construction. Putnam (1995) provides a flavor of this attitude: "[The] revolt against formalism is not a denial of the utility of formal models in certain contexts; but it manifests itself in a sustained critique of the idea that formal models. . .describe a condition to which rational thought either can or should aspire" (p. 63).

Thus, a basic claim of commonsense realism is that previous efforts, by empiricists, idealists, and realists alike, were misguided in seeking a formal, logical solution to the enduring problems that have plagued the philosophy of science. This formalism, we believe, has led to misconstruing both the goal and process of human sensemaking. Harre described the relevant issues in terms of two fallacies: "Contemporary sceptics have slipped into the commission of the 'philosophers' fallacy.'. . .By their defining, even only tacitly, such cognitive phenomena as scientific knowledge in terms of truth and falsity, the demands placed on a community which has the task of accumulating some of 'it' are set in such a way that 'it' can never be achieved. . . .[Second, the] giving of primacy to logical structures as the inner essence of discourse has had a disastrous effect in philosophy of science" (1986, p. 4).

Harre's first point implies that, instead of holding that the goal of inquiry and theory development is to establish the truth value of various claims, neo-realists hold that the goal is to allow judgments about the plausibility of these claims. Indeed, this is the central epistemological point that differentiates neo-realist theories from previous realist positions. No human theory has avoided revision in the face of continued inquiry, and no final theory is expected. Dropping ultimate "truth" as the goal of inquiry does not, however, equate with sanctioning *any* conclusion. Rather, there are criteria to be used to support conclusions, as we discuss later, but universal or absolute truth will not be the goal.

With respect to the process of inquiry, Harre's second point—that giving "primacy to logical structures. . .has had a disastrous effect in philosophy of science"—emphasizes that it is fallacious to believe that human understanding is or should be based on formal logic. Again, sensemaking, which refers to our evolved capacities to make sense of the world in ways that support effective action, becomes a more appropriate alternative to formal logic. But how are we to take advantage of our natural strengths in sensemaking and compensate for our weaknesses? We address these issues within the remaining themes of emergent realism.

Contextual Complexity. Building on the commonsense notions of causal regularities and naturalized epistemology, emergent realism presumes that the knowledge questions of interest to evaluators are conditioned by our understanding of the contexts of social programs.

Nature of Reality: Context-Sensitive Mechanisms and Causal Regularities. Two aspects of reality are presumed to direct natural sensemaking in a complex world. First, consistent with the open systems perspective that has developed in the past fifty years, emergent realists expect that causal processes will be sensitive to contextual influences. For example, programs that cause particular effects in one context may yield different effects in other circumstances (Bunge, 1997). Accepting this notion of open systems with context-sensitive mechanisms, evaluators turn from the question, Is the program effective? to the more textured question, For whom is the program effective, with what program elements, and under what conditions?

This emphasis on contextual influences runs counter to contentions that evaluators should simply estimate aggregate "program effects." We reject the assumption of context-invariant effects implicit in this approach. But we equally reject the claim by others that reality is so contextually complex and undifferentiated that there are no meaningful regularities to observe. Instead, the second aspect of reality that drives realist sensemaking is the belief that our world is sufficiently differentiated, with underlying mechanisms, that at least some of the patterns revealed by proper inquiry do have implications beyond the particular context in which they were observed. Indeed, were it not for such implications—for the usefulness of generalizing beyond the data observed—why would we, as humans, have evolved our elaborate sensemaking capacities? Decisions about how to deal with context-sensitive mechanisms require judgments about the value of increased specificity. While we recognize the worth of going beyond purely aggregate conclusions about program impacts, reasonably confident and useful answers can be developed about the impacts of similar programs on identified groupings of individuals, even allowing for some variation in the accompanying conditions.

Nature of Understanding: Evolved Ways of Knowing. The emergent realist alternative is based on the belief that, having evolved in a complex, open systems world, humans have evolved "ways of knowing" (Tharp, 1981) appropriate for such a world. We contend in the following discussion that (1) sensemaking is not the deductive process envisioned in the validation paradigm, (2) induction is not the discredited activity that some would claim, and (3) retroduction is an important part of a naturalized theory of causal understanding.

1. Deduction. Popper rejected confirmation of deductions as a sound basis of knowledge and emphasized instead the use of falsified predictions to discredit theories. In this sense, both positivism and Popper's falsificationism depend on deduction and, more specifically, on constant conjunction as the criterion for supporting causal claims: If constant conjunction is not necessary, failure to observe constant conjunction—or something close to it (Popper recognized that a single failure rarely justified discarding a theory)—could not lead to falsification of the theory that generated a disconfirmed hypothesis.

The realist critique of deduction points out that, in an open systems world, it is unrealistic to expect that a given mechanism will always yield the same result and, thus, that there will be a constant conjunction of cause and effect. For example, in the open systems in which evaluators work, there are innumerable alternative potential influences that often moderate how presumed causal mechanisms manifest themselves as observed patterns. We have limited capacity to be sensitive to such complexity, and even those moderating effects that we can recognize may be further moderated by other contextual factors (Cronbach, 1975). If we understood completely the impact of the moderating influences, we would be able to refine our predictions to retain the essence of constant conjunction, but such complete knowledge is unlikely in open systems

(House, 1991). Emergent realist "laws," therefore, are not required to manifest themselves in terms of constant conjunction of observed phenomena, but rather as *tendencies,* general patterns of causal relations that may vary as a function of other, often unknown, influences. As a result, strict deduction has its limits.

2. Induction. The inadequacy of deduction as a foundation for developing causal laws is particularly discouraging if one rules out an important role for induction in establishing valid knowledge, as some logical empiricists did. Newer forms of realism, on the other hand, do not dismiss humans (in everyday life or in systematic inquiry) as incapable of accurate induction.

Defining induction as the movement from specific facts to general conclusions (Reese, 1980, p. 251), some studies, consistent with Campbell's "evolutionary epistemology" (1974b, 1977), have presented psychological evidence that supports the existence of an evolved capacity for induction in humans (Kornblith, 1993). For example, children appear to induce underlying categories, sorting objects by natural kind rather than by superficial similarity (Gelman and Markman, 1986). Even research that casts doubt on humans' inductive ability may in its own way strengthen the realist position. For example, Nisbett and Ross (1980) found that individuals are not good at induction when shown 2 x 2 contingency tables and asked to estimate the degree of covariation between two variables, particularly when they have prior beliefs about the relationship between the variables. However, consistent with the realist belief in evolved capacities, better evidence for induction is found in more natural settings—more akin to the complex settings in which human induction evolved—where, in contrast to being given only 2 x 2 contingency tables, people have clusters of properties to support inductive inference (see, for example, Kornblith, 1993, p. 101).

3. Sensemaking as retroduction: Causal pattern matching. We contend that evaluators should attempt to identify causal mechanisms that are responsible for observed patterns. While this active construal of causality can be represented as the result of some combination of induction and deduction, many realists follow the lead of pragmatists such as Pierce in using *abduction* or, more commonly today, *retroduction,* to describe "the process of starting with anomalous facts and ending with explanatory hypotheses" (Reese, 1980, p. 491).

If retroduction occurs within an iterative process, in which our initial explanatory hypotheses guide our efforts to gather appropriate "facts," which then support more refined hypotheses, and so on, we describe something akin to the sensemaking model promoted by Weick (1979). According to this model, the sensemaking process involves three components, or subprocesses: enactment, selection, and retention. *Enactment* refers to the actions humans take in creating and bracketing a subset of the population of possible experiences. For example, asking respondents to fill out a questionnaire results in behaviors that otherwise would not have occurred. *Selection* represents the interpretation process by which meaning is given to the bracketed experience by applying and selecting among available interpretative templates. Modern social scientists have vast repertoires of templates available for making sense of social phenomena; our current templates include concepts such as authority and power, alienation, empowerment, and open systems, only some of which presumably were available in centuries and millennia past. Finally, *retention* refers to the process by which the choices regarding enactment and selection that lead to effective action are retained for use in similar situations. This retention can be valuable despite our claim that, in a sufficiently complex context, the patterns observed through sensemaking will be emergent relative to predictions based on available templates. Progress can be an outcome of the process, not in the sense of attained truth, but in the sense of having more adequate patterns and enactment activities with which to approach subsequent patterns (Weick, 1979). Campbell (for example, see 1974, 1977), in his descriptive epistemology, gives a similar model.

Hierarchical Reality. Along with most critical realists (such as, Bhaskar, 1979), emergent realists believe that the context-sensitive mechanisms just described are part of a reality that is stratified in levels, in the sense that observed regularities are the result of unobserved underlying causes. Thus, unlike positivists who viewed constant conjunction between identified causes and effects as the evidence of true explanation, neo-realists have focused on what are referred to as underlying generative mechanisms.

Nature of Reality: Stratified Causal Orders. As a simple example of the neo-realists' conception of the stratified nature of reality, imagine that we heat a volume of gas sealed in a container. We would observe that the increase in temperature is associated with an increase in pressure. Underlying what we observe, however, are physical interactions of the gas molecules such that the increased heat causes increased activity of the molecules and thereby increases pressure. Thus, we can talk about causality on a more molar level (describing heat and pressure changes in a mole of gas) or on a more molecular level (specifying the interactions of individual molecules). Social phenomena can likewise be conceived. For example, Pogge (1995) identifies a molar-molecular distinction in two traditions of social justice research, one that conceives the mechanisms of causation (and moral responsibility) at the molar level of social institutions, and another that emphasizes more molecular causes at the level of interpersonal interactions.

Nature of Understanding: Nested Causal Explanations. One significant implication of the multilevel structure of reality is that the causal relations we seek to understand cannot be directly observed. It is as if we are trying to understand the relations among a team of underwater divers by observing the relations among the bubbles that rise to the surface. (Although employed to different effect, this is the essence of Plato's metaphor of a man chained near the mouth of a cave who tries to understand the relationships of real life by observing the shadows of life visible on the cave wall.) This stratified nature of reality has led some to argue that real understanding requires molecular analyses. Thus, some scientific realists (inappropriately, we believe) deny the import of everyday observations while emphasizing scientific analysis of more molecular levels: "Physics has discovered that the table is mostly empty space. . . .The reaction of Wilfrid Sellar's [scientific realism] is to deny that there are tables at all as we ordinarily conceive them" (Putnam, 1987, p. 3).

Two noteworthy complications arise, however, in claiming the fundamental superiority of molecular analyses. First, whatever unit of analysis one is using can always be decomposed into ever more molecular units and, similarly, any underlying generative mechanism that has been identified can itself be subjected to ever more molecular analyses. For example, in the case of the heat-volume relationship for gas, the level of analysis could become even more molecular by examining the activities of the subatomic particles that underlie the relationships among the gas molecules. For an example of an underlying generative mechanism being subjected to ever more molecular analyses, consider an evaluation of the effect of surveillance video cameras on auto thefts. Potential criminals' assessment of the probability of being arrested may be identified as the underlying mechanism responsible for the cameras' crime-reduction effect (Pawson and Tilley, 1997). Additional, more molecular, analyses could then be conducted—for example, studying differences in the personalities or learning histories of those criminals who were and those who were not deterred by the cameras—to identify why this deterrent mechanism operated for some would-be criminals but not others. In principle, these increasingly molecular analyses could continue toward the study of neurological mechanisms underlying program impacts, and even beyond.

A second objection to exclusively molecular analyses arises from the obvious value of molar analyses in everyday life (Meehl, 1986, p. 319). Molar models often provide value and efficiency in communication. More fundamentally, when a precise understanding of the interactions of the molecular dynamics is necessary but absent—as we expect in the social sciences—molar phenomena are emergent from, and not readily extrapolated from, the predictions of more reductive theories. Hence, emergent realism maintains that everyday sense-making should not be replaced by more molecular, scientific analyses, but rather should be enhanced by them.

This focus on nested causal explanations suggests that Weick's sense-making model can be extended to address the multiple levels of a stratified reality. Harre (1986) and Aronson, Harre, and Way (1995) provide a model that begins to capture the multiple levels represented in good theory. According to Aronson, Harre, and Way, "the content of a theory consists of a set of paired models. One of the pair serves to represent the phenomena to be explained while the other represents the mechanism by which those phenomena are generated" (1995, p. 51). Of course, the state of affairs for researchers is even more complicated than suggested by Harre's two-model system, in that explanatory accounts can be attempted at multiple levels (for instance, social structural, interpersonal, psychological, neuropsychological), and multiple explanatory accounts can be applied at any particular level (as when an evaluator of training considers self-efficacy, implicit knowledge, commitment, and other accounts at the individual, psychological level). Given this complexity, and given that theory (including program theory) should include at least the two types of models noted by Harre, the plausibility of a particular theory "is not measured [simply] by degree of correspondence with the facts, nor is it an expression [simply] of the degree of coherence of the theory in question with other theories. Relative (im)plausibility assessments partake in some measure of each" (Harre, 1986, p. 215; also see Campbell, 1991).

Based on the preceding arguments, emergent realism takes a middle ground between those who emphasize molecular analysis and those who resist efforts at reductionism. Moreover, emergent realism contends that, while the appropriateness of any level of analysis is dependent on the context, understanding will typically be enhanced by a combination of molecular and molar analyses. In evaluation, the assessment of the most appropriate levels of analyses generally depend on utilization—and increasingly molecular analyses may not enhance utility.

Emergent Order. The last theme of emergent realist evaluation we introduce here is incorporated into the name of the approach. It originated in evaluation in such concepts as the "Emergentist Principle" of Campbell (1974a), whose work on evolutionary epistemology is not as widely known among evaluators as his contributions to methodology. Whereas the prior two themes provided explanations for emergent phenomena based on underlying mechanisms, emergent order refers to the emergent phenomena that result from the high levels of evolved organic complexity that characterize the phenomena of interest to biologists and, even more so, to social scientists. As we will see, this emphasis on emerging order is in stark contrast with the positions dominant within the validation and interpretivist paradigms.

Nature of Reality: Emergent Evolutionism. Campbell's emergentist claim is that "biological evolution. . .encounters laws, operating as selective systems, which are not described by the laws of physics and inorganic chemistry. . .[nor by their] future substitutes" (Campbell, 1974a, and cited in Munro, 1992, p. 119). That is, evolution, because of the dynamics of organic interactions, has produced biological and social phenomena of increasing complexity that resist explanation in terms of more mechanistic forms of analysis. For example, we view human social interactions as complex phenomena that are not captured by the laws of Newtonian mechanics.

This emergentist claim highlights a point of conflict between logical empiricists and constructivists, with the former envisioning a unified reality explained reductionistically, and the latter focusing on subjective meaning purportedly not amenable to the methods of the validation paradigm. The concept of emergent phenomena might seem to support the constructivist side of this controversy, since it represents the antithesis of the positivist dream of reductionism. However, it presents a very different sort of problem for constructivists, who reject the notion of "progress" implicit in emerging order. To accept that our current understanding is more advanced than it was in the distant past (be it 100 or 10,000 years ago) is to admit that some notions are more warranted than others.

Nature of Understanding: Metaphors of Sensemaking. Human sensemaking, we believe, evolved in a world characterized by different levels of emergent order. Consistent with this evolutionary perspective, recent research in cognitive psychology suggests that humans have "autonomously evolved [capacities, or] . . . domain-specific competencies" (Sperber, 1996, p. xviii) appropriate for these different levels. What are the characteristics of our evolved, domain-specific competencies? They appear to be strikingly similar to what we would expect given the rhetoric of the validation-interpretivist paradigm wars and the integration of the emergent realist approach: "At this point, the evidence . . . strongly points to at least two sets of explanatory biases corresponding to two conceptual domains: a physical-mechanical domain that helps explain . . . mechanical causality, and a folk psychological domain that helps explain . . . belief-desire accounts of causation" (Keil, 1996, p. 243).

Supporting Emerging Order. We can use the notion of emerging order to help make sense of the increasing complexity of social programs and of the role that they, and evaluation, play in society. As Julnes and others (1987) suggest, such concepts as "assisted performance" and "scaffolding" (Bruner, 1978), which are based in Vygotsky's (1978) developmental theory, provide a view of the role of social programs: to assist the performance of those whom they serve.

This notion of assistance does not imply a patriarchal view of program clients being guided by others with more wisdom; to the contrary, most recent work in this area has emphasized that the social supports referred to as scaffolding are joint productions of everyone involved in the social activities. The metaphor of a tree being supported by a scaffold of posts and wires is thus extended, with the tree contributing to the very scaffolding that then supports it (and with the scaffolding-induced growth yielding new scaffolding to further guide the process). Also, unlike the scaffolding provided by a benevolent gardener, the socially-constructed scaffolding of emergent realism requires no firm understanding of the eventual endpoint of the process—it is only necessary that the scaffolding processes that effectively support growth are employed more often than those processes that are less effective.

Given this developmental perspective, we judge evaluations as less adequate to the extent they neglect explicit attention to the impacts of programs on social developmental processes. Sensemaking's role, therefore, is not merely to support warranted actions in the immediate context of the evaluation, but also to support the emerging process of knowledge construction, that is, enlightenment.

Implications for Evaluation Methodology

We have described emergent realism as an alternative paradigm that is better able to support the knowledge construction activities of evaluators. But what specifically does emergent realism imply for methods of knowledge construction? We have in other arenas discussed a number of connections between realist theories of knowledge construction and practical inquiry (Julnes, 1995; Mark, 1996; Mark, Henry, and Julnes, in preparation). In this section we summarize some general implications of an emergent realist approach for evaluation methodology.

Context-Sensitive Inquiry. It is not earthshattering to suggest that the methods an evaluation employs should fit the context of the specific evaluation. As indicated in Chapter One, emergent realism goes beyond this generality by suggesting that the types of fit are important. First, the choice of which levels of molarity to examine should be context-sensitive. It is appropriate, for example, to argue from physiological principles to behavior in one context and adopt corresponding methods (such as, measuring dosage prescribed and self-reports in drug evaluation trials), and yet also to argue from sociological principles to individual behavior with corresponding methods in other contexts (such as, measuring the impact of programs designed to reduce road-rage among urban drivers).

Second, the level of aggregation that is used in one's inquiry and conclusions should be context-sensitive. As just noted, logical empiricists attempted to reach general conclusions that applied to all people under all circumstances, whereas radical constructivists appear to reject the meaningfulness of all aggregated conclusions. The neo-realist reconciliation involves the recognition that all aggregated conclusions can themselves be disaggregated into more refined claims, but that this further specificity may not be valuable. To the emergent realist evaluator, judgments about the right level of specificity are based not on some general philosophical principle, but on context-specific judgments about utility.

In these and other ways, emergent realism can help guide method choice. An important determinant of emergent realist method choice is the nature of our knowledge about the mechanisms likely to operate in a specific context. We use the terms *competitive elaboration* to describe procedures appropriate when one begins (a phase of inquiry) with an explanatory model in mind, and *principled discovery* to describe procedures that are not driven by a priori explanatory models. After describing these as though they were distinct, we briefly discuss their integration.

Competitive elaboration. Competitive elaboration refers to the process by which alternative explanations—whether alternative program theories or validity threats—are ruled out (Reichardt and Mark, 1998). To carry out competitive elaboration, one first specifies the implications of a possible mechanism so as to discover any implications that conflict with those of alternative mechanisms (including validity threats). One then collects data that allow an assessment of whether the implications of the mechanism or those of its competitor hold true. In other words, when an explanatory account is susceptible to alternative explanation, the plausibility of the alternative—and of the original—can be put to test by adding a comparison that places the explanatory account and the alternative explanation into competition (for examples, see Mark, 1990; Mark, Hofmann, and Reichardt, 1992; and Reichardt and Mark, 1998).

As Chapter One notes, competitive elaboration can be accomplished through a variety of research designs, including moderated multiple regression, analysis of variance, hierarchical linear modeling, meta-analysis, and qualitative observation. In competitive elaboration, such techniques would be used for planned analyses to assess causal mechanisms by determining whether observed program effects vary as predicted by one's hypothesized underlying generative mechanism across different client subgroups, settings, outcome variables, treatment variations, or time lags. In addition, research on mediating processes can also be used to carry out competitive elaboration: Different generative mechanisms are likely to imply different mediational chains, so a test of mediation will usually meet the requirements of competitive elaboration.

Principled Discovery. Bhaskar (1989b), in considering the implications of open systems, emphasized the importance of theory tests that did not involve traditional, a priori, theory-derived predictions: "Particularly important here will be the capacity of a theory to be developed in a non-ad hoc way so as to situate, and preferably explain [a finding]. . .when it could never, given the openness of the social world, have predicted it" (p. 83). The realist perspective presented in this chapter likewise emphasizes that the confirmationism of the empiricist approach is often unrealistic given the complexities of the open systems for which social science models are prepared. Thus, we are confronted with a dilemma: We want a methodology that is (1) appropriate for the complexities of open systems yet (2) still provides a mechanism by which we can discipline the conclusions that result from our efforts at interpretation. The term *principled discovery* implies that there are methods that can allow for discovery, via induction, in the complexities of an open system, but are principled in that they are disciplined by data and are not simply post hoc explanations of chance observations.

Central to principled discovery is the iteration between induction and deduction that takes place once the inquiry has begun. Smith (1997) provides a fine example, from an interpretivist tradition, of the iterative process of inducing an explanatory account from a set of observations, and then disciplining the account by a search for confirming and disconfirming evidence. Alternatively, Tukey's (1977) exploratory data analyses, other graphical methods (Henry, 1995), and even traditional quantitative techniques such as regression used in an exploratory fashion (Tukey, 1977) can lead to worthwhile discoveries. For example, it might be shown that effects are larger for one client group than for others, or that larger effects tend to occur in one treatment setting. To be principled, such observations should initiate attempts to specify and test an underlying mechanism that would account for them. Even tests of variance shifts can instigate a discovery that can be disciplined with additional data (Mark, 1996).

Context-Confirmatory Inquiry. Context-confirmatory inquiry is one important emergent realist way of integrating competitive elaboration and principled discovery (Julnes, 1995). It is a context-specific application of the iterative sensemaking model: Based on the expected inquiry context, deduced implications of potential underlying mechanisms are identified and used to guide our choice of methods; data are gathered to evaluate the initial hypotheses (via competitive elaboration) and to induce more complex patterns, especially regarding underlying generative mechanisms, in the actual context of the inquiry (via principled discovery); the newly hypothesized generative mechanisms are then used as the basis for other, distinct predictions; and these new predictions are then tested (via competitive elaboration), initially with other elements of the original data set, and then with new data, as necessary and feasible. The rallying cry for the context-confirmatory approach is, One never knows so little that competitive elaboration should not be initiated; one never knows so much that principled discovery is redundant.

Context-confirmatory inquiry integrates the induction of the interpretist paradigm and the deduction of the validation paradigm, yielding a form of causal pattern matching that some realists refer to as retroduction. This integration of induction and deduction in context-confirmatory inquiry is not unique to either the quantitative or qualitative approach (or to mixed methods). Indeed, Yin (1989, pp. 214–215) has described a similar integration in the context of the iterative process that guides case study research, and such iterative integration involves one aspect of what is referred to as the hermeneutic circle (Balfour and Mesaros, 1994, p. 560).

In addition to its integration of induction and deduction, the context-confirmatory approach facilitates integration of molecular and molar causal perspectives. As with the hermeneutic circle, understanding the interaction of the parts of a system helps one understand the whole; conversely, understanding the whole helps in understanding the parts. The more molar perspective on causality is associated with aggregate, summative statements, which may be necessary for decision making. The more molecular perspective is associated with underlying mechanisms (and hence mediation) and with disaggregated estimates of impact (and hence moderation). Taken together, these give a foundation for assessment of merit and worth, and for choices about program revisions. In addition, the molar and molecular perspectives support each other: Improved molecular analyses support the validity of more molar assessments (by reducing the plausibility of alternative explanations), whereas molar assessments provide the overall patterns to be explained by improved molecular accounts.

Conclusion

Emergent realism, we believe, represents a potential rapprochement in the paradigm wars that have taken place in evaluation and elsewhere. It also provides a foundation for current exemplary practice in evaluation and suggests further directions for practice. Epistemological and ontological foundations of emergent realism—including common-sense realism, contextual complexity, the hierarchical structure of social phenomena, and the emergentist principle—argue for (1) an evaluation methodology that gives priority to the study of generative mechanisms, (2) attention to multiple levels of analysis, and (3) mixed methods appropriate for our evolved capacities. Although not emphasized in this chapter, choices about when and how to mix methods, as with other methods choices, can be based on the emergent realist desire to (1) discover underlying mechanisms, (2) discipline such speculations with data, (3) elaborate our understanding through multiple levels and multiple metaphors, and (4) provide credible evidence to potential evaluation users. In addition, the realist principles developed here are compatible with the emphasis in emergent realism on values (see Chapter Three). Further, they also can be applied to other activities that evaluators undertake, such as monitoring and classification (Mark, Henry, and Julnes, in preparation).

References

Aronson, J. L., Harre, R., and Way, E. C. *Realism Rescued.* Chicago: Open Court, 1995.

Balfour, D. L., and Masaros, W. "Connecting the Local Narratives: Public Administration as a Hermeneutic Science." *Public Administration Review,* 1994, *54,* 559–564.

Bhaskar, R. A. *A Realist Theory of Science.* Leeds, U.K.: Leeds Books, 1975.

Bhaskar, R. A. *The Possibility of Naturalism.* Hemel Hempstead, U.K.: Harvester, 1989a.

Bhaskar, R. A. *Reclaiming Reality.* New York: Verso, 1989b.

Bruner, J. "The Role of Dialogue in Language Acquisition." In A. Sinclair, R. J. Jarvella, and W.J.M. Levelt (eds.), *The Child's Conception of Language.* New York: Springer-Verlag, 1978.

Bunge, M. Mechanism and Explanation. *Philosophy of Social Sciences,* 1997, *27,* 410–465.

Campbell, D. T. "Downward Causation in Hierarchically Organised Biological Systems." In F. J. Dobzhansky and A. Dobzhansky (eds.), *Studies in the Philosophy of Biology.* Berkeley, CA: University of California Press, 1974a.

Campbell, D. T. "Evolutionary Epistemology." In P. A. Schilpp (ed.), *The Philosophy of Karl Popper.* La Salle, Ill.: Open Court, 1974b.

Campbell, D. T. *Descriptive Epistemology: Psychological, Sociological, and Evolutionary.* William James Lectures. Cambridge, Mass., 1977.

Campbell, D. T. "Coherentist Empiricism, Hermeneutics, and the Commensurability of Paradigms." *International Journal of Educational Research,* 1991, *15,* 587–597.

Cook, T. D., and Campbell, D. T. *Quasi-Experimentation: Design and Analysis Issues for Field Settings.* Boston: Houghton Mifflin, 1979.

Cronbach, L. J. "Beyond the Two Disciplines of Scientific Psychology." *American Psychologist,* 1975, *30,* 116–127.

Drake, D., and others. *Essays in Critical Realism.* London: Macmillan, 1920.

Feigl, H. "Positivism in the Twentieth Century (Logical Empiricism)." In Weiner, P. P. (eds.), *Dictionary of the History of Ideas.* New York: Scribner, 1973.

Gelman, S. A., and Markman, E. M. "Young Children's Inductions from Natural Kinds: The Role of Categories and Appearances." *Child Development,* 1986, *58,* 796–804.

Gergen, K. "Social Psychology as History." *Journal of Personality and Social Psychology,* 1973, *26,* 309–320.

Guba, E. C. "The Alternative Paradigm Dialog." In E. C. Guba (ed.), *The Paradigm Dialog.* Newbury Park, Calif.: Sage, 1990.

Harre, R. *Varieties of Realism.* Oxford: Blackwell, 1986.

Henry, G. T. *Graphing Data: Techniques for Display and Analysis.* Newbury Park, Calif.: Sage, 1995.

House, E. R. "Realism in Research." *Educational Researcher,* 1991, *20,* 2–9.

Julnes, G. "Context-Confirmatory Methods for Supporting Disciplined Induction in

Post-Positivist Inquiry." Paper presented at the 1995 conference of the American Evaluation Association, Vancouver, British Columbia.

Julnes, G., and others. "The Process of Training in Processes." *Journal of Community Psychology,* 1987, *15,* 387–396.

Keil, F. C. "The Growth of Causal Understandings of Natural Kinds." In D. Sperber, D. Premack, and A. Premack (eds.), *Causal Cognition.* Oxford: Oxford University Press, 1996.

Kornblith, H. *Inductive Inference and Its Natural Ground.* Cambridge, Mass.: MIT Press, 1993.

Mark, M. M. "From Program Theory to Tests of Program Theory." In L. Bickman (ed.), *Advances in Program Theory.* New Directions for Program Evaluation, no. 47. San Francisco: Jossey-Bass, 1990.

Mark, M. M. "Social Programming as a Sense-Making, Value-Staking, Human Enterprise: Toward a Model of Social Programming for Neo-Realist Evaluators." Paper presented at Essex '96: Meeting of the International Sociological Association Methods Division, 1996.

Mark, M. M., Henry, G. T., and Julnes, G. "Evaluation, A Realist Approach: Monitoring, Classification, Causal Analysis, and Values Inquiry." in preparation.

Mark, M. M., Hofmann, D., and Reichardt, C. S. "Testing Theories in Theory-Driven Evaluations: (Tests of) Moderation in All Things." In H.-t. Chen and P. H. Rossi (eds.), *Using Theory to Improve Program and Policy Evaluations.* New York: Greenwood Press, 1992.

Meehl, P. "What Social Scientists Don't Understand." In R. A. Schweder and D. W. Fiske (eds.), *Metatheory in Social Science: Pluralisms and Subjectivities.* Chicago: University of Chicago Press, 1986.

Mohr, L. B. *The Causes of Human Behavior.* Ann Arbor, Mich.: University of Michigan Press, 1996.

Munro, D. "Process Use Structure and Levels of Analysis in Psychology: Towards Integration Rather Than Reduction of Theories." *Theory and Psychology,* 1992, *2,* 109–127.

Nisbett, R., and Ross, L. *Human Inference: Strategies and Shortcomings of Social Judgment.* Englewood Cliffs, N.J.: Prentice-Hall, 1980.

Pawson, R., and Tilley, N. *Realistic Evaluation.* Thousand Oaks, Calif.: Sage, 1997.

Pogge, T. W. "Three Problems with Contractarian-Consequentialist Ways of Assessing Social Institutions." In E. F. Paul, F. D. Miller, and J. Paul, *The Just Society.* Cambridge: Cambridge University Press, 1995.

Popper, K. (1968). *The Logic of Scientific Discovery.* New York: Harper Torchbooks.

Putnam, H. *The Many Faces of Realism.* LaSalle, Ill.: Open Court, 1987.

Putnam, H. *Realism with a Human Face.* Cambridge, Mass.: Harvard University Press, 1990.

Putnam, H. *Pragmatism.* Oxford, U.K.: Blackwell, 1995.

Putnam, H. *Representation and Reality.* Cambridge, Mass.: MIT Press, 1996.

Reese, W. L. *Dictionary of Philosophy and Religion.* Atlantic Highlands, N.J.: Humanities, 1980.

Reichardt, C. S., and Mark, M. M. "Quasi-Experimentation." In L. Bickman and D. J. Rog (eds.), *Handbook of Applied Social Research Methods.* Thousand Oaks, Calif.: Sage, 1998.

Shadish, W. R., Cook, T. D., and Leviton, L. C. *Foundations of Program Evaluation: Theories of Practice.* Newbury Park, Calif.: Sage, 1991.

Smith, J. K., and Heshusius, L. Closing Down the Conversation: The End of the Qualitative-Quantitative Debate Among Educational Inquirers. *Educational Researcher,* 1986, *13* (1), 4–12.

Smith, M. L. "Mixing and Matching: Methods and Models." In J. C. Greene and D. J. Caracelli (eds.), *Advances in Mixed-Method Evaluation: The Challenges and Benefits of Integrating Diverse Paradigms.* New Directions for Evaluation, no. 74. San Francisco: Jossey-Bass, 1997.

Smith, M. L. "Qualitative plus-versus Quantitative: The Last Word." In C. S. Reichardt and S. F. Rhallis (eds.), *The Qualitative-Quantitative Debate: New Perspectives.* New Directions for Program Evaluation, no. 61. San Francisco: Jossey-Bass, 1994.

Sorokin, P. *Social and Cultural Dynamics.* Boston: Porter Sargent, 1957.

Sperber, D. "Introduction." In Sperber, D., Premack, D., and Premack, A. (eds.), *Causal Cognition*. Oxford: Oxford University Press, 1996.

Tharp, R. G. "The Metamethodology of Research and Development." *Educational Perspectives*, 1981, *20*, 42–48.

Tukey, J. W. *Exploratory Data Analysis*. Reading, Mass.: Addison-Wesley, 1977.

Vygotsky, L. S. *Mind in Society*. Cambridge, Mass.: Harvard University Press, 1978.

Weick, K. E. *The Social Psychology of Organizing*. New York: Random House, 1979.

Yin, R. K. *Case Study Research: Design and Methods*. Newbury Park, Calif.: Sage, 1989.

In this chapter, realist principles frame evaluation as a support for democratic processes in the pursuit of social betterment. Social betterment is defined as the extent to which public policies and programs meet the ever-emerging complex of human needs. Distinct implications for the practice of evaluation, including balancing among values, analyzing distributional aspects of a program, and informing democratic processes are discussed.

Values and Realist Evaluation

Gary T. Henry, George Julnes

Evaluation begins with the presumption that some social conditions are preferable to others. Less homelessness is better than more. Higher levels of reading comprehension are preferred to lower levels. Work is preferable to welfare. Such presumptions seem necessary to justify value judgments, and they appeal to our commonsense experience. Yet no theory of values seems adequate. We are left wanting a defensible base for our value claims, but finding no firm foundations. Recent generations of evaluation have promoted two primary responses to the dilemma just posed: Empiricists with positivist leanings rejected the centrality of value issues and restricted themselves to factual claims; radical constructivists found no justification for one value system over another and so asserted that all value claims are equally valuable. In this chapter we critique these two positions and offer a realist alternative.

The difficulty with the first position (logical empiricism) is that it avoids an inherent aspect of evaluation. Avoiding issues of values results in value choices influencing evaluations in often unacknowledged ways. For example, evaluators apply their sensemaking skills to identify whether a policy has altered pre-existing conditions and how. The conditions on which an evaluator chooses to focus, however, are not all of the benefits and problems that are plausibly associated with the policy. The choice of focal conditions legitimates some outcomes at the expenses of others, giving greater weight to the interests of those who value the chosen conditions.

Constructivist evaluators do not avoid value issues, but rather make them central to the task of evaluation. Bringing values into evaluation theory is essential (they were never absent from practice, even if only implicit), but doing so raises controversies that always accompany value issues. Once values are recognized as central but not objectively determined, practicing evaluators are forced to justify their activities and their interpretations against claims from other value positions. The added accountability and fairness that result from a more self-reflective approach to values is an important development in evaluation, but the lack of consensus on values can lead practicing evaluators into a thicket of controversies and multiple, competing value positions. It is fine to advocate multiplism, but we are left with nagging questions: "How can results from diverse criteria, methods, measures, and stakeholders be combined?" (House, 1995, p. 33).

In this chapter, we discuss the realist alternative by first developing in the value arena the anti-formalism that was presented in Chapter Two for knowledge construction, pointing out false dichotomies that have limited the contributions of earlier formal theories of values. Then, using the same three realist themes that were applied to knowledge construction, we outline an alternative realist view of valuing as a natural social activity that can be supported, but not replaced, by evaluation. In the final section of this chapter, we make explicit some of the implications of the ER perspective on values for the practice of evaluation.

Impediments of Formalism

The anti-formalism that was responsible for many of the insights developed for knowledge construction performs much the same function for a theory of valuing. Just as formal theories of knowledge were presented as not receptive to lessons from experience, so too has this formalism been a source of controversies that have distracted us from a better understanding of natural valuing. In particular, we contend that the past emphasis on formal theories of valuing resulted in evaluation suffering from three impediments to making value choices in an evaluation, impediments which we pose as three false dichotomies: First is the fact-value distinction. Second is the formalism-relativism trap. Third is the inevitable versus illusory perspective on social progress. These three impediments have hindered the recognition that humans have a natural capacity for valuing aspects of everyday life as well as issues of policy.

Beyond the Fact-Value Dichotomy. The first impediment to gaining a firmer foothold on values questions is the attempt to exempt factual conclusions from being burdened by values issues. The typical claim is that facts and values represent distinct claims with little or no overlap. The key to understanding the negative effects of this fact-value dichotomy is the recognition that both empiricists and constructivists have presumed that value claims are inherently subjective. Wanting objectivity, traditional "[s]ocial scientists avoided value issues, claiming they could only determine causal claims" (House, 1995, p. 46). Constructivists, committed to the centrality of seemingly subjective value judgments, emphasized the subjectivity of purported factual claims about causality and so were driven to embrace relativism (Schwandt, 1997).

A third alternative is to follow the lead of realists such as Putnam who see facts and values as intrinsically intertwined without that entanglement necessarily leading to relativism. Putnam points out that those with opposing ideologies and policy positions are just as likely to disagree on the facts as on the criteria used to judge the worth of a policy (1990, p. 190). Yet Putnam also claims, as we will develop later, that it is possible to put forth nonarbitrary values, just as it is possible to make justified causal claims. Thus, we believe that it is possible to develop a reasoned stance on values in evaluation despite their presumed subjectivity and despite the recognition that our theories about the world influence our values and our values influence our evaluation activities.

Absolute versus Relative Values.   Once values are recognized as necessary for evaluation, the first instinct of many is to attempt a formal justification for treating one's preferred value as fundamental. It is as if having an absolute value that is fundamental in all circumstances is necessary to justify our actions. Not surprisingly, the variety of theories promoting one value or another tend to conflict. For example, naive utilitarian values that would justify seeking efficient resource allocation may conflict with moral values, such as honor, dignity, or truth. Libertarian values that give the highest weight to individual rights may square off against the social conservative position that stresses policing and social controls (Etzioni 1996, pp. 160–165). The most common overreaction to these less than satisfactory values conflicts is the profound relativism developed by some radical constructivists that views all values as arbitrary and the choice of any particular one as a matter of individual preference. This relativistic stance seems to lead to an anything-goes rule for practice. Fortunately, a third alternative exists.

Realism presents the belief that formal theories founded on particular values are important in developing our expectations and in framing a critical analysis of potential values positions, but they are rarely adequate to serve as the sole or primary foundation for practice. Chapter Two developed the claim that knowledge construction follows from natural sensemaking rather than from formal logic. In the context of valuation, realists' anti-formalism rejects claims that we can or should follow any particular single, formal theory in making value judgments. As such, we do not begin with a "sweeping principle" to which adherence is a litmus test for an evaluator's morality or immorality (Putnam, 1990, p. 181). Instead, we recognize that evaluators, like government officials, can find themselves in situations where an action is exactly right in utilitarian terms and exactly wrong in moral terms (Tong, 1987) with no formal means of reconciling the conflict. In our opinion, House (1995, p. 45) provides a useful summary of the realist response to formalism: "use of formal philosophic theories, such as Rawls's (1971) theory of justice, can serve to inform and critique our positions but need not be used to determine judgments in every evaluation, or how certain interests should be weighted in advance of the study." Rather than attempt to "prove" the validity of a particular value stance that applies in all contexts, we will offer natural valuation as the emergent realist solution to restoring a sense of balance to value judgments. The path to natural valuation must, however, continue to remove impediments. This time we confront the issue of social progress and begin to set our sights on the ER purpose for evaluation.

Promoting Social Betterment. We will tether emergent realist evaluation securely to a belief in social improvement that includes a non-utopian view of social progress (Putnam, 1995). This reflects the same sentiment that earlier evaluators have expressed. For instance, in his reflections on twenty-five years of practice as an evaluator, Covert states, "we chose to be evaluators so that we could contribute to making the world a better place" (1995, p. 42). Evaluation findings can serve to enlighten, inform, or guide decisions about policies and programs that are themselves collective attempts to improve social conditions.

Despite the commonsense appeal of viewing evaluation in support of making the world a better place, the notion of progress is at the center of yet another controversy in our field, a controversy that we believe is fueled by yet another artificial dichotomy. In this case, the dichotomy places evaluators in one of two camps: Either you believe in an inevitable progress of society as defined by some set of universal values, or you believe that progress is illusory and only in the eyes of the beholders. The appeal of universal values finds its way into a utopian view of social progress, which always leads to contradictions in making internally consistent decisions or in running roughshod over an important but excluded value (See Putnam's, 1987, discussion of Huxley's *Brave New World*).

Inability to pose a set of universal values, such as equality or justice, as moral guideposts has given rise to the belief that progress is an illusion. In educational reform, it is easy to see that an exclusive interest in improving aggregate performance *could* lead to greater inequities between the privileged and the disadvantaged. Progress on one dimension *could* worsen another, leading to the conclusion that progress is an illusion. However, the relationship between performance and inequities is not a logical necessity just because it is possible. And the conclusion omits another logical, if difficult, possibility. Overall performance can improve by raising the performance of the disadvantaged and reducing the gap between them and the privileged (See Glymph and Henry 1997, for an analysis of the impact of minority performance gaps on aggregate performance). This sense of balance between values is an important aspect of natural valuation.

We will elaborate this position in the following discussion on the notion of emergent order, but here we stress that, by using the term *non-utopian,* we admit that social progress is notoriously difficult to define in that it is not inevitable nor is it likely to be completely comprehensible in terms of any current value system. Nonetheless, we reject claims that improvement is not possible or that it is impossible to intentionally support this sort of progress. Indeed, we suggest that it is the belief in the possibility of progress, difficult as it is to define, that is responsible for the myriad stances on the use of evaluation in support of social policy, from economic perspectives that emphasize movement toward Pareto optimality, to notions of empowerment, and even to critical analysis of human emancipation. Leaving until later the discussion of how evaluation findings may actually translate into changes in social policy (see Henry and Rog, Chapter Five of this volume), we cling to the necessity of the possibility of social betterment as the preeminent rationale for evaluation as we offer our perspective on natural valuation.

Natural Valuation

The first step in developing a realist theory of values is to recognize that we make value judgments every day in choosing some activities over others (Putnam, 1995). This experience of everyday valuing reminds us that valuation is a natural activity, adaptive and important despite our apparent inability to capture its complexity in formal theories. In a manner similar to Chapter Two on knowledge construction, we propose to draw on three aspects of a realist's view of social reality in building our theory of ERE valuation: contextual complexity; stratified nature of reality, sometimes referred to as embedded systems; and emergent processes. Our purpose in employing these principles in the discussion of values is that we believe that they account for important insights from past practices and can be used to inform future practice.

Contextual Complexity. We saw in Chapter Two that central to most of the neo-realist theories of the past half-century has been a belief in the contextual complexity of phenomena. Many assert that, with regard to evaluation, the impacts of programs are contextual in the sense that they depend on the characteristics of the services that are delivered, of the people receiving the services, and of the communities in which the programs are offered. This complexity inhibits general predictions to other sites because the conditions that inform the predictions are never replicated in exact detail.

If the impacts of programs are contextual, then so are value judgments about the programs. Here, contextual means that the value of a program is contingent on a variety of factors. As we noted in our critique of formalism, some would use this contextual complexity to insist on a dichotomy between value positions: either you believe in universal values that apply equally well regardless of context, or you contend that value judgments vary profoundly across people and circumstances. And as with impacts, emergent realism rejects the extremism implied in these two positions and instead presents a third alternative. On the one hand, ER evaluators recognize that different types of people, living in different communities, will experience different social circumstances and are likely to see value in different outcomes. On the other hand, taking the contextualist position to its extreme conclusion would mean that evaluations would have to address the value judgments of every individual affected by a program or policy, and further, would take into account that those judgments change over time.

Thus, realist valuation is not so simplistic as to suggest universal values or a summing of individual values into a social welfare function, but neither is it so ambiguous as to entail radical relativism. Whereas contextual complexity argues against universal values, there are meaningful patterns in our social world such that warrant value judgments. "We are not committed to the existence of an unimaginable 'absolute perspective' in ethics, an ethical theory that contains and reconciles *all* the possible perspectives on ethical problems in all their dimensions; we *are* committed to the idea of 'better and worse opinions'" (Putnam, 1990, p. 183). This balanced approach, which recognized the legitimacy of different values held by different people yet believes that we can be justified in using these different values to derive more general value judgments, is supported by a range of realist evaluators. Speaking about the position presented by Shadish, Cook, and Leviton (1991), House (1995, p. 44) notes that, "We agree that the values and interests of important stakeholder groups can and should be included in an evaluation, that the evaluator can and should make syntheses, and that the evaluator should not use formal theories of justice in a routine, a priori manner."

Having argued for an anti-formalist approach to valuation that requires a balanced interpretation of the implications of contextual complexity, we next discuss two ways in which the value of a program is contingent on contextual factors. The first contingency involves the balance between different individuals or communities, and the second involves the balance between different values.

Balance Among Individuals. One of the major problems in justifying social programs is that programs that benefit some almost always entail costs to others (Gramlich, 1990). Evaluators could ignore the distribution of costs and benefits and adopt the Kaldor-Hicks criterion of program value, estimating the overall value as a function of the net present value of aggregated benefits minus costs. Or evaluators could choose a naive Rawlsian approach and address only the impact of the programs on the least advantaged.

But most people, regardless of political persuasion, fall somewhere between the Rawlsian and the Kaldor-Hicks positions. Most do believe that the distribution of program effects is often relevant in judging overall value, but most also agree that the value we place on equality is not absolute. A program that benefits the poorest Americans would be valued differently by most from a program that, otherwise identical, benefits the richest Americans. Nonetheless, a program that pursued equality solely by reducing the opportunities for those of above-average wealth would generate little support. For example, an evaluative judgment of the value of a publicly funded educational TV program such as *Sesame Street* will be influenced by the value one places on helping children in families with limited resources. To the extent that one cares at all about helping those less advantaged, assigning a value to the program requires an understanding of the characteristics of the children reached by such a program and the characteristics of those who derive the greatest program benefits. Cook and others (1975) illustrate the contextual subtleties in valuating programs such as *Sesame Street:* although the program had a positive overall impact on the cognitive development of the children who watched, its impact was greatest on children in higher socioeconomic groups (whose parents would later build on what was covered during the program), thus increasing the gap between those with greater and lesser resources. The aggregate effect, or net effect, was positive, so the evaluator operating with this as the sole criterion would have missed this differential impact. To the extent that we care about equality, and thus distribution of program impacts, we need to perform analyses that identify distributional consequences.

Balance Among Values. In addition to achieving balance in a program's effects on different individuals, emergent realist evaluation also recognizes that context influences the choice of effects to be studied. We can illustrate this contextual aspect of valuing by contrasting the Kaldor-Hicks criterion with Rawls' equality criterion. Where Kaldor-Hicks uses efficiency as the primary value in evaluation, a Rawlsian account assigns value to programs and policies based on their impact on those who are least advantaged. Many debates have addressed whether efficiency or equality should be more fundamental in the evaluation of social programs. Rather than take sides in this debate, ERE contends that the relative value assigned to a social value such as efficiency or equality is itself contextual. The economic concerns of the 1980s led to more vigorous promotion of efficiency and less promotion of equality than during the more prosperous 1960s.

This position on the relative priority of values has an established history in policy analysis, going back to Okun's (1975) trade-off between equity and efficiency. Indeed, even the meaning of such values is contextual; as Wildavsky (1991, p. 149, emphasis deleted) points out, "what is efficient for people who prefer one way of life may not be efficient for people who value a different culture." Fainstein (1987) provides an example of a contextual analysis of the priority of values in her analysis of the conflict between the efficiency argument of private urban developers and the equity argument of those seeing their communities displaced by development.

To summarize, we have argued that the notion of contextual complexity gives evaluators the responsibility to consider the impacts of programs and policies in terms of a balance of values rather than in terms of a single foundation. As Schwandt (1997) notes in his review of the role of values in evaluation in the past decade, attaching evaluation to a formal set of moral principles has never withstood the dissecting scalpel wielded by social philosophers. Though our philosophy does not have the dash of the pursuit of a pure ideal such as equality, social justice, liberty, or human emancipation, we offer this realist alternative in the belief that letting go of absolute values makes it easier to discern areas of meaningful value convergence (House, 1995, p. 44). The task for practicing evaluators is to identify and balance differences in values and differences among individuals that arise out of specific contexts.

Stratified Nature of Reality. Part of the rationale for a contextual view of values is provided by the realist's recognition of the stratified nature of reality. Recall that stratification can be understood as a reality comprised of nested levels of systems: an individual can be analyzed in terms of embedded physiological systems, but the individual is embedded in a family system which, in turn, is embedded in larger social groupings (Haldane, 1996). Further, realists assert that the effects found at one level typically cannot be reconstructed from the more molecular dynamics (see Julnes and Mark, Chapter Two). Therefore the mechanisms through which long-term effects can be produced lead to valuing immediate outcomes that are associated with different strata. Individual behaviors are not inconsistent with the chemical processes and biological wiring studied by neuropsychologists, but they are not entirely accountable in terms of those molecular processes (Bouchard, 1997). For example, recent studies show the importance of stable, caring social relationships in the brain development of very young children (Bogley, 1997). If we believe in this stratification and want to promote social progress, we need to value program impacts at each system level.

One concern is that unless multiple levels of impacts are considered, evaluators may miss the real value of a program. As Heflinger (1992, p. 32) points out for mental health evaluation, a "client-level focus on outcomes . . . is needed in addition to treatment- and system-level foci in order to determine the effects of mental health interventions." Similarly, evaluating the Head Start program using standardized test scores as the sole criterion of success may limit the evaluation unnecessarily by neglecting the changes in children's social environments that may influence positive outcomes in the future. For example, program-induced changes in the expectations of parents, their interactions with their children, and the educational resources they make available for their children's development may all affect the long-term cognitive and social development of the children. The program may also affect teachers' evaluation of the children by improving the children's social behaviors or the teachers' assessment of the children's abilities; the teachers' expectations or assessments could legitimate a higher status in school and increase the resources made available for these children. Thus, if the long-run hopes for the Head Start program are pinned to providing better life chances for children from the least advantaged families, the mechanisms through which this might occur exist at more than one level, often with impacts at one level enhancing or negating impacts at other levels (see Lee and Loeb, 1995, for an example of how school environment can erode individual gains).

The stratified nature of reality gives rise to another value issue. If individuals, families, communities, and states are given standing as legitimate entities, the interests of these embedded entities can differ and even be in conflict from one level to another. For example, the HOPE scholarship program provides college tuition and fees for Georgia high school graduates earning a cumulative GPA of 3.0 or better in high school to attend college in the state. This may increase the human capital in the state by increasing the number of college-educated residents. Colleges and universities selected by HOPE scholarship recipients benefit from the enrolment of better-prepared students. However, students who might have enrolled in a more appropriate school out-of-state may actually have their choice of colleges limited by the economic incentives to stay in Georgia. Some colleges that previously attracted high-performing local students because of the students' income constraints might lose these students to distant schools that the students find more desirable. And, of course, other states lose the better Georgia students who otherwise would have gone out of state. The level of analysis chosen—individual, school, state, or nation— makes a difference for the interpretation of the value of the same outcome. For some evaluators, this could force a choice between the individual level and one or more levels of the community, such as the school or the state. The realist, however, does not choose between one level and another but makes a commitment to recognize these stratified levels: "to adapt a formula of Hilary Putnam's, 'the person and society jointly make up the person and society'" (Haldane, 1996, p. 71). Multilevel assessments may create problems for synthesis, but greater problems will result from simple assessment of only one level of the stratified reality.

Emergent Processes. Values emerge. They emerge over time through the evolution of human needs, and they emerge in our time as a result of analysis and critical examination. We address both of these aspects of emergence to develop our view of how evaluators can conduct their craft without feigning to be value-neutral or claiming to possess the correct values.

Need-Based Valuation. To say that values have evolved is to argue that they are adaptive in meeting human needs. "It is because there are real human needs, and not merely desires, that it makes sense to distinguish between better and worse values, and, for that matter, between better and worse knives" (Putnam, 1987, p. 79). This argues against relativism in that some values are claimed to be more effective in guiding behaviors that meet real human needs: it is not the case that everyone's values are equally valid. Evaluation, if it is to contribute to social betterment, should help us understand how programs and policies are meeting real needs.

This evolutionary view of need-based values, however, also rejects efforts to reduce values to a single value, be it a moral value such as equality or a physical need identified for lower organisms. Rather, we have an evolved hierarchy of needs and associated values: "Dewey, like Goodman, tells us that human needs also do not pre-exist, that humanity is constantly redesigning itself, and that we *create* needs" (Putnam, 1987, p. 79). Further, we create these needs and the values that address them for a reason; we believe this emergence occurs because values operate not as a formal ethical logic but rather as scaffolding that supports our natural movement toward development and betterment. We used the scaffolding notion earlier when we discussed knowledge construction, and use it here in the same sense of providing the support necessary for proper development. As we develop, our needs change and the needed scaffolding changes.

This conception of an evolved hierarchy of values helps to reconcile the debate between those who assess programs using quantitative measures of benefits and costs and those who emphasize moral values. The evolutionary aspect of realism argues that the naive utilitarianism underlying many benefit-cost analyses is appropriate for more basic needs, and the moral critiques of critical theory are appropriate for more complex human needs that continue to evolve. At this point in human development, one of the more complex needs deserving attention in evaluation is our need for a moral image of our world.

Putnam (1987) describes a moral image of the world as "a picture of how our virtues and ideals hang together with one another and of what they have to do with the position we are in" (p. 51). Moral images are available from many alternative sources; for example, Etzioni's (1996) *New Golden Rule* provides a well-articulated image of improvement based in communitarianism. Although differing moral images are available, if this developmental view is taken seriously, evaluation must find ways to bring these moral images to bear on efforts to valuate programs and policies. Democratic processes provide a justified mechanism for identifying and applying these moral images in evaluation.

Emergence Through Democratic Processes. Believing that human needs have evolved and continue to evolve highlights a second task for a theory of valuation, realist or otherwise, to address—establishing a program's or policy's value to society. Rejecting both relativism and absolutism, many realist theories advocate representational democracy as a valuating mechanism. Democratic processes provide the overall judgments that would otherwise have to be modeled in an overly complicated way. Hurley (1989) argues that democratic institutions are more likely than other arrangements to lead to "the truth about what should be done" (p. 349). But she also argues that democracy "is a way of realizing as well as discovering what ought to be the case" (1989, p. 349).

Hurley's arguments are founded on the primacy of, but not absolutist adherence to, individual autonomy. Because there are no formulas for valuation, no absolutes to provide firm guidance, individuals are autonomous in the sense of judging value issues for themselves. The role of evaluation in such a society is to provide the feedback necessary for informed decision-making in representational democracy. Evaluation, therefore, does not *decide* the merit of a social policy. Instead, evaluation functions as a social support that *informs* democratic processes concerning social betterment. Thus we can link evaluation to the goal of social progress without having a complete a priori definition of what social progress is.

Emergence Through Evaluation. A policy or social program is set up to solve or ameliorate a "social problem" that has resulted from some ongoing social processes (Kingdon, 1995; Hilgartner and Bosk, 1988; Mark and Henry develop this point in Chapter Four of this volume). Given that the values expressed in the process of defining a social problem and its solution have emerged through democratic processes such as legislative debates, citizen panels, or administrative action, it is not surprising that early evaluators attached themselves to these values in designing their evaluations. However, the initially sanctioned values are always subjected to further scrutiny, sometimes as a direct result of the evaluations, and often other values are voiced and subsequently incorporated into evaluations. In his seminal work on issue networks, Heclo (1978) identifies the growth of a community that is attached by intellectual and emotional interests to the debates over policy and the values served by particular policies rather than by the material benefits associated with the policies (also see Kingdon, 1995). Critical debates over values are grist for the policy communities' mills.

In a very real sense, values emerge as we give more focused attention to explicit social objectives, unanticipated consequences, and implementation issues. For example, evaluations of early childhood education programs such as Head Start began by focusing on the cognitive development of the children as the criterion for merit of the program (McKey, 1985). But as findings showed that the cognitive gains dissipated with passing years whereas the social benefits to the children continued (Barnett, 1995), the social outcomes for disadvantaged children took on more importance. In reworking the objectives, it became clear that improving the life chances for these children, not promoting cognitive gains, was the ultimate goal. Cognitive gains were a potential means to an end, but they were not the only means to valued social outcomes. Parents interacting with their children, educational resources within the home and during school, and teacher expectations were also identified as potential mechanisms for achieving the valued end, improving the children's social outcomes (Entwisle, 1995; Alexander and Entwisle, 1996). As the mechanisms that might result in long-term, positive outcomes for the children were better understood (cognitive development representing only one among several), the immediate objectives of the program were changed, broadened, and subjected to evaluation and critical review (See Wilson 1994 for an example of the latter). A better understanding of the mechanisms that must be triggered to produce desired outcomes from a program can cause new values to emerge as important intermediate outcomes and can also cause the ultimate outcomes to be modified. Experience with a program can identify negative products or by-products as well. For example, the structure of welfare was often associated with the increase in out-of-wedlock births among the poor and was blamed for creating economic dependence (Murray, 1984). Having values emerge through analysis and social interaction is, based on the ER perspective, a good thing that is to be supported as we seek to achieve social progress.

In summary, EREs believe there is no formal theory of values to guide us, only a reasoned perspective that our needs, and with them our values, have evolved. These evolved values guide us in working toward social improvement through democratic institutions. Evaluation is framed as a support for informing our natural valuation capacities, often involving democratic processes, and thus contributing to the long-run move toward social betterment. The realist principles of contextual complexity, stratified nature of reality, and emergent order all have implications for conducting evaluation in pursuit of social betterment. Evaluation practice must take advantage of the commonsense understanding of the process of valuation without losing direction in the confusion of values that constitutes relativism, or stumbling due to the blinders of "value-free" science.

Implications for Practice

We have presented valuation as a natural process central to formal evaluation and to most other human activities. The realist account just developed suggests that the role of evaluation is to support this natural process and that properly doing so will contribute to social betterment. Much of the evaluation currently done is indeed contributing to this desired progress, but in this section we will sketch out two implications of our realist principles that are somewhat unique. These are practical options that we believe should be more widely applied by practicing evaluators. ERE supports the notion that, in evaluation, inquiry into values is as important as sensemaking activities. To support this belief, we recommend two aspects of realist evaluation: supporting context-contingent valuation and supporting stratified valuation.

Supporting Context-Contingent Valuation. The contextual complexity seen by realist evaluators makes it a virtual certainty that different people will experience different needs, many not immediately obvious at first blush to evaluators. Balancing the needs of different individuals in an evaluation helps extend the natural valuation process into more formal evaluation. Failure to incorporate the proper range of needs risks bias in the assessment of outcomes. For example, in examining the impact of the Family Cap provision, which denies additional welfare benefits when a woman has another child while on welfare, numerous criteria might be chosen. Measuring the impact of program changes on live births and family size follows from a different sense of human needs than does assessing the impact on the well-being of the children in the family. Established procedures for adding balance to the focal outcomes involve stakeholders.

Stakeholders as a Source of Balance. Given the current fragmentation of evaluation methods, the term *stakeholder* is used in a variety of ways. Patton, for whom stakeholders are the lynchpin of his "utilization-focused evaluation," offers the following definition that seems to capture the essence of what most mean by stakeholders: "Stakeholders are people who have a stake—a vested interest—in evaluation findings. For any evaluation there are multiple stakeholders: program funders, staff, administrators, clients, and others with a direct, or even indirect, interest in program effectiveness" (1986, p. 43). Patton further insists that stakeholders are specific people—those individuals who are likely to use information. But this emphasis on specific people is not made in many other definitions. For most evaluations, stakeholders are identified from groups to provide advice on how an evaluation is to be conducted and interpreted.

Stakeholder selection in the more general use of the term is beset with questions of who represents a group, how should they be incorporated into the evaluation, who has decision-making authority, how should their involvement be maintained, and whose interests take priority. ER evaluators accept that the desired balance resists formal identification, and they try to develop methods of value inquiry that will reveal the comprehensive configuration of values. However, these configurations are not directly accessible in their natural state. All methods or evolved technologies for revealing the complex of competing values are flawed and contain potential biases, just as they are with sensemaking methods.

Stakeholder groups are often organized by evaluators to provide opinions about values to be incorporated into an evaluation. One method of doing this is by organizing focus groups that provide input to the evaluators at the beginning of an evaluation. In some cases, these are one-shot activities, not an ongoing involvement with the evaluation. In other cases, the evaluation is informed throughout by a group of stakeholders who might have some direct responsibilities for parts of the evaluation or who might offer advice or make decisions about the evaluation. Even more formally structured methods of involvement are being used by evaluators to elucidate and balance the value choices (Idris and Eichelberger 1997).

Limitations of Stakeholder Involvement. With any method, the selection of individuals for participation is a crucial decision for the evaluation and the acceptance of the findings. It is not easy to decide who speaks for teachers, nor is it easy to decide who speaks for welfare recipients. Deliberate heterogeneity can be useful to better understand dissenting opinions, but pre-existing power relationships can quell the debate. Homogeneous groups can increase participation within the groups, but they can also lead to strong biases in the opinions delivered to the evaluators, at worst, or to extremely localized opinions that have not been nourished by the quality of democratic debate possible with more heterogeneous groups. That is, no method for selecting and organizing the groups is without some problems. Our values-related techniques and technologies have been developed to respond to particular omissions or problems in our vision of values, and therefore all are fallible. This is not to dismiss them all, but rather to suggest that all have utility within the bounds of their inherent limitations. For ER evaluation, deliberative discussion within the context of a democratic society, as suggested by Dewey and Habermas, is an ideal, but only proximal methods are possible for an evaluation. Surveys, focus groups, and stakeholder processes are all imperfect means for a deliberative discussion of the merits of a public program, but they are all tools that allow greater inclusion in conducting an evaluation. They provide additional perspectives, but, for ER evaluators, no single method provides the ideal perspective. While humbling, the limitation is also a strength. It provides the ER evaluator with a reason for critically analyzing the outputs of these processes, rather than being a captive of them.

Identifying Contextual Variation. The preceding analysis of stakeholders makes clear that realist valuation is affected by the distributional consequences of the program. ER practice seeks ways to better support our natural valuation of distributional allocations. Our basic claim is that it is possible and desirable for evaluation reports both to reduce complex relationships into summary form and also to represent some of the complexities that convey the richness of context necessary for natural valuation.

If we accept that the value of a program is influenced by its distributional consequences, then we want our methods to provide an understanding of these consequences. The *Sesame Street* example illustrates the importance of going beyond aggregate impacts in assigning value to a program; contextual factors such as the characteristics of those best served by the program do matter. This recognition of the impact of contextual factors on program outcomes is a central feature of ERE and thus influences the methodology used to evaluate programs. ERE emphasizes these distributional issues by advocating analysis of moderated relationships with regard to equality. As Julnes (1994) points out, such an analysis can be conducted with qualitative or quantitative methods. An example of a quantitative method is the inclusion of interaction terms (created by multiplying one variable by another and treating the product as a separate variable) in regression analysis. By including an interaction term based on multiplying program participation by a measure of poverty, the regression analysis would allow us to report program impacts as a function of poverty.

One argument against analyzing moderated relationships, an argument often defended by reference to Cronbach (1975), is that there are many potential moderated relationships to study (including higher-order interactions) and no fundamental reason to study some over others. The example of Sesame Street, however, illustrates the ERE claim that a consideration of context need not result in an infinite regression of ever more subtle contextual influences; Cook and others (1975) did not look to see if program impacts were moderated by such contextual factors as the size of the family television set or the number of hours of sunlight experienced by the children. Each of these contextual factors could have an influence on program effectiveness, but they were not examined because (1) we have every reason to believe that their causal impacts on program effectiveness are likely to be small relative to the moderated effect associated with socioeconomic background, and (2) contextual effects that are not related to differential socioeconomic advantages, such as hours of sunlight, are of less concern for the valuing component of evaluation. An ER evaluation, therefore, looks for contextual influences but does so within realistic limits and with regard to the value-relevance of the influences.

Supporting Stratified Valuation. Some evaluators have responded to the dilemma of balancing the interests of stakeholders, and at the same time have bypassed the problem of selecting for representativeness, by giving priority to a particular set of stakeholders' interests. House (1995), for example, recommends a contextual Rawlsian approach and determines that evaluation should speak for the poor and disenfranchised, who have no voice otherwise. Empowerment evaluation goes further to advocate evaluation as a tool for empowering specific groups who exercise little influence within current institutional arrangements. Both of these approaches are consistent with the needs-based grounding of realist valuation, but both also take a different turn than traditional stakeholder involvement by including overarching values (such as equality or human dignity) rather than a balance among stakeholders. Such overarching values can be justified by the existence of embedded systems.

The realist principles presented above argue for a stratified view of our social world: individuals are embedded in the larger social entities of families, communities, and societies. Each of these levels is recognized in emergent realism and is allowed standing in debates over the proper balance of values used to guide public policy. This recognition that family, community, and societal values may not coincide with those of identified individual stakeholders requires evaluators to take special care to include these system-level values. For realist evaluators, system levels are emphasized by a firm commitment to treating the "public" as a stakeholder. We also find promise in a parallel analysis for incorporating family values, but this topic is beyond the scope of this chapter.

Public as Stakeholder. The stratified world of emergent realism includes social systems, such as communities or larger societies, with values that cannot be derived from linear combinations of individual values. In this world, the "public," referring to a particular social entity, is a stakeholder in public policy issues. Heflinger (1992) makes this point for mental health programs: "Three major stakeholders in mental health outcomes, each holding unique perspectives on the goals of mental health intervention, are the client, the mental health professional, and society at large" (p. 32). This, we argue, is the almost totally neglected aspect of evaluation that takes place within a pluralist democracy—valuing the opinions and attitudes of the public. That is, the public expresses choice on social policy issues—directly through elections and indirectly through public opinion surveys—yet the public's views are almost totally ignored in conducting evaluations (Henry, 1996). Both the freshness of this perspective and its controversy can be seen in the American Evaluation Association's "Guiding Principles for Evaluators," which refers to the public interest and "the welfare of society as a whole", (Shadish, Newman, Scheirer, and Wye, 1995b), as well as in the attention this statement has garnered in subsequent discussions of the principles (Shadish, Newman, Scheirer, and Wye, 1995a; House, 1995; Covert, 1995; Schwandt, 1997).

We are not, however, arguing that there is a single public interest. In a complex social reality, members of the public hold certain and sometimes widely different attitudes about public programs. Some of these values may be weakly held by small minorities, some strongly held by large majorities. These values, just as those of individual stakeholders, policy-makers, and evaluators, need to be incorporated into evaluations. Although MacDonald (1976) has labeled some evaluations as "democratic," these appear to be democratic in the sense of *corporate democracy,* giving standing to individuals based on their role in the program being evaluated. This corporate conception of democracy is entirely distinct from the representational, one person–one vote variety of democracy that is most common in developed nations. The role of representative democracy, however, is fundamental to ER evaluators, given the high value placed on autonomy and, therefore, on democratic institutions. Although we could justify the importance of the public from the standpoint of use of the information (see for instance Kingdon's discussion of the importance of the "national mood," 1995), we see the public as fundamental to the view that evaluation supplies information to democratic processes.

Once we accept the importance of including the public as a stakeholder, however, an important related question arises: Who represents the public?

Although this is a nasty problem for many stakeholder groups—for instance, who represents teachers?—it is particularly acute for the public. For stakeholders such as teachers, organizations are often used to represent their particular views, but organized citizen groups are usually more likely to represent a special-interest perspective than some notion of the general public. Can we say that a governor's appointee represents the public? How about the citizen who decides to show up at a public hearing? We argue that the difficulties in selecting representatives of the public is another important reason for treating the public as a separate and distinguishable group, one whose values need to be given outside of the more routine stakeholder involvement methods.

With ERE's goal of evolutionary human progress, the unfilled information gap of the public's opinions and values is often too large to be ignored. Henry (1996) has detailed three ways information from public opinion surveys can be used for evaluation: framing the questions to be addressed in the evaluation; exposing myths or incorrect beliefs about a program; and assessing the level of public support or opposition for potential evaluation recommendations. The first type of public involvement can help frame the evaluation questions, including the outcomes to be addressed, by providing the public's views on the purpose of the program or their expectations for the program's success. We can illustrate giving voice to the public in this way with an example using public and other stakeholder group surveys.

In the ongoing longitudinal evaluation of Georgia's pre-kindergarten program available to all four-year-olds in the state, general population surveys were used in combination with surveys of parents of participants, pre-K teachers, and program administrators. Potential reasons for offering the program and expectations for its outcomes were stratified into three levels: child related, family related, and state related. Probability samples were taken from three of the four stakeholder groups, and all program administrators in the central office were asked to rate the three lists that had been stratified by level. These ratings were used to discover both consensus and conflicts in outcome preferences and concerns for negatively perceived outcomes. The results have been incorporated into plans for measuring specific outcomes during the twelve-year evaluation and in reporting results most relevant to each group. For instance, social interactions between children was a pre-eminent expectation for parents. The first report of site observations spoke to social interactions and other child-centered beliefs and practices. In information releases to the public, the evaluators stressed issues of importance to the public, including developmentally appropriate activities, as opposed to free day care for the preschoolers.

Evaluation in Support of Democratic Processes. The issue of reporting raises another important point about including the public in an evaluation. Research has shown that large segments of the public have inaccurate information about many aspects of social programs (Kull, 1994, 1995; Elam, Rose, and Gallup, 1996; Henry, 1996). Normatively, we want and expect a public armed with informed opinions. However, we must ask, What is the role of ER evaluation in informing the public? When viewed as a support for informing democratic processes, the importance of informing the public as a part of evaluation reporting is clear. However, evaluation reporting is primarily targeted for specific groups of stakeholders, including sponsors and those who may have instrumental uses for the findings. Hence, the public is often not presented with evaluation findings. Again from the ER evaluation perspective, we argue for a broad distribution of information, especially using efficient channels for informing the public, that is, the media. Informing the public at the end of an evaluation may lead to better informed opinions at the beginning of the next evaluation cycle. In this way, we can support representative democratic processes by reporting results to the range of relevant stakeholders, to legislators, to executives and administrators, to clients, and to the public, all of whom have valuable roles in discovering and realizing society's progress.

Summary

The general framework of emergent realism has allowed us to develop a particular view of making value judgments in evaluation. In this view, the value we place on programs depends not only on distributional concerns for such value-based concepts as equality and efficiency, but also on the context. Given this dependence on context and the complexity in analysis that it entails, we are left without a prescription for assigning values to social programs. The inability to prescribe in advance the most desirable set of outcomes for any particular program, brings us back to the importance of democratic processes for raising concerns and criticism about the desirability of the outcomes that result from the program. But we must keep track of the importance of democratic institutions, and their managers and administrators, in meeting human needs. Thus, emergent realist valuation ties itself to the concepts of emerging definitions and understanding of human needs and, hence, to the principles underlying representational democracy as a means for defining and realizing social progress.

References

Alexander, K., and Entwisle, D. "Educational Tracking During the Early Years: First-Grade Placements and Middle-School Constraints." In A. Kerckhoff (ed.), *Generating Social Stratification: Toward a New Research Agenda.* Boulder, Colo.: HarperCollins, 1996.

Barnett, W. "Long-Term Effects of Early Childhood Programs on Cognitive and School Outcomes. *The Future of Children,* 1995, 5 (3), 25–49.

Bogley, S. "How to Build a Baby's Brain." *Newsweek,* 1987, Spring-Summer, 28–32.

Bouchard, T. J. "Whenever the Twain Shall Meet." *The Sciences,* 1997, 37 (5), 52–57.

Cook, T. D., and others. *"Sesame Street" Revisited: A Case Study in Evaluation Research.* New York: Russell Sage Foundation, 1975.

Covert, R. W. "A Twenty-Year Veteran's Reflections on the Guiding Principles for Evaluators." In W. Shadish, D. Newman, M. Scheirer, and C. Wye (eds.), *Guiding Principles for Evaluators.* New Directions for Program Evaluation, no. 66. San Francisco: Jossey-Bass, 1995.

Cronbach, L. J. "Beyond the Two Disciplines of Scientific Psychology." *American Psychologist*, 1975, *30*, 116–127.

Dewey, John. *Democracy & Education: On Introduction to the Philosophy of Education.* New York: The Free Press (1966).

Elam, S.M., Rose, L.C., and Gallup, A.M. "Phi Delta Kappa/Gallup POLL of the Public's Attitudes Toward the Public Schools." *Phi Delta Kappan*, 1996, *78* (1) 41–58.

Entwisle, D. "The Role of Schools in Sustaining Early Childhood Program Benefits." *The Future of Children: Long-Term Outcomes of Early Childhood Programs*, 1995, *5* (3), 133–144.

Etzioni, A. *The New Golden Rule: Community Morality in a Democratic Society.* New York: Basic Books, 1996.

Fainstein, S. "The Politics of Criteria: Planning for the Redevelopment of Times Square." In F. Fischer and J. Forester (eds.), *Confronting Values in Policy Analysis.* Newbury Park, Calif.: Sage, 1987.

Glymph, A., and Henry, G. T. "How Well Did Schools Perform?: Simpson's Paradox and Analyzing Outcomes," New Directions for Evaluation, no. San Francisco: Jossey-Bass, 1997.

Gramlich, E. M. *Benefit-Cost Analysis for Government Programs.* (2nd ed.) New York: McGraw-Hill, 1990.

Habermas, J. "Between Facts and Norms: Contributions to a Discourse Theory of Law and Democracy." Cambridge, MA: MIT Press, 1996.

Haldane, J. "The Individual, the State, and the Common Good." *Social Philosophy and Policy*, 1996, *13*, 59–79.

Heclo, H. "Issue Network and the Executive Establishment." In A. King (ed.), *The New American Political System,* 1978.

Heflinger, C. A. "Client-Level Outcomes of Mental Health Services for Children and Adolescents." In L. Bickman and D. Rog (eds.), *Evaluating Mental Health Services for Children.* New Directions for Program Evaluation, no. 54. San Francisco: Jossey-Bass, 1992.

Henry, G. "Community-Based Accountability: A Theory of Accountability and School Improvement." *Phi Delta Kappan,* 1996, *78,* (1), 85–90.

Hilgartner, S., and Bosk, C. "The Rise and Fall of Social Problems: A Public Arenas Model." *American Journal of Sociology,* 1988, *94* (1), 53–78.

House, E. R. "Putting Things Together Coherently: Logic and Justice." In D. Fournier (ed.), *Reasoning in Evaluation: Inferential Links and Leaps.* New Directions for Evaluation, no. 68. San Francisco: Jossey-Bass, 1995.

Hurley, S. *Natural Reasons: Personality and Polity.* New York: Oxford University Press, 1989.

Idris, H., and Eichelberger, R. "Using the Knowledge Use System to Improve Evaluation in the Egyptian Ministry of Education." A paper presented at the American Evaluation Conference, November 1997.

Julnes, G. "Pursuing Equity in Evaluation Conclusions: Importance of Analyzing Moderated Relationships." Paper presented at the conference of the American Evaluation Association, Boston, Mass., 1994.

Kingdon, J. *Agendas, Alternatives, and Public Policies.* (2nd ed.) Boston: HarperCollins, 1995.

Kull, S. *Fighting Poverty in America: A Study of American Public Attitudes.* Washington, D.C.: Center for the Study of Policy Attitudes, 1994.

Kull, S. *Americans and Foreign Aid: A Study of American Public Attitudes.* Washington, D.C.: School of Public Affairs, 1995.

Lee, V., and Loeb, S. "Where Do Head Start Attendee's End Up? One Reason Why Preschool Effects Fade Out." *Educational Evaluation and Policy Analysis,* 1995, *17* (1), 62–82.

MacDonald, J. B. "Evaluation and the Control of Education." In D. Tawney (ed.), *Curriculum Evaluation Today: Trends and Implications.* London: Macmillan, 1976.

McKey, R. *The Impact of Head Start on Children, Families, and Communities.* Washington, D.C., 1985. (ED 263984)

Murray, C. *Losing Ground: American Social Policy, 1950–1980.* New York: Basic Books, 1984.

Okun, A. M. "Equality and Efficiency: The Big Trade-Off." Washington, D.C.: Brookings Institution, 1975.

Patton, M. *Utilization-Focused Evaluation.* Beverly Hills, Calif.: Sage, 1986.

Putnam, H. *The Many Faces of Realism.* LaSalle, Ill.: Open Court, 1987.

Putnam, H. *Realism with a Human Face.* Cambridge, Mass.: Harvard University Press, 1990.

Rawls, J. *A Theory of Justice.* Cambridge, Mass.: Belnap Press of Harvard University, 1971.

Schwandt, T. A. "The Landscape of Values in Evaluation: Charted Terrain and Unexplored Territory." In D. Rog and D. Fournier (eds.), *Progress and Future Directions in Evaluation: Perspectives on Theory, Practice, and Methods.* New Directions for Evaluation, no. 76. San Francisco: Jossey-Bass, 1997.

Shadish, W., Cook, T., and Leviton, L. *Foundations of Program Evaluation: Theories of Practice.* Newbury Park, Calif.: Sage, 1991.

Shadish, W., Newman, D., Scheirer, M., and Wye, C. "Developing the Guiding Principles." In Shadish, W., Newman, D., Scheirer, M., and Wye, C. (eds.), *Guiding Principles for Evaluators.* New Directions for Program Evaluation, no. 66. San Francisco: Jossey-Bass, 1995a.

Shadish, W., Newman, D., Scheirer, M., and Wye, C. (eds.), *Guiding Principles for Evaluators.* New Directions for Program Evaluation, no. 66. San Francisco: Jossey-Bass, 1995b.

Tong, R. "Ethics and the Policy Analyst: The Problem of Responsibility." In F. Fischer and J. Forester (eds.), *Confronting Values in Policy Analysis.* Newbury Park, Calif.: Sage, 1987.

Wildavsky, A. "Efficiency as a Function of Culture". In A. Wildavsky (ed.), *Administration in Social Work.* Berkeley, Calif.: Hayworth, 1991.

Wilson, J. Q. "Culture, Incentives, and the Underclass." In Aaron, H. J., Mann, T. E., and Taylor, T (eds.), *Values and Public Policy.* Washington, D.C.: Brookings Institution, 1994.

Social programming is an evolved mechanism for addressing social needs (among other things). Evaluation focuses largely on social programs. We review selected aspects of the complex dynamic, political, and contextual factors that influence social programming, and from these we draw conclusions about the conduct of emergent realist evaluation.

Social Programming and Policy-Making: A Realist Perspective

Melvin M. Mark, Gary T. Henry

The field of evaluation today largely remains focused on program evaluation. Program evaluation, of course, is fundamentally concerned with social policies and programs. Nevertheless, many early writers about program evaluation gave relatively little attention to the nature of social policy-making or programming (Shadish, Cook, and Leviton, 1991). This inattention was unfortunate, because implicit or explicit beliefs about the nature of social programming and policy-making influence the ways evaluators define their purpose, approach their tasks, design and carry out evaluations, communicate their findings, and seek to facilitate use (Shadish, Cook, and Leviton, 1991; also see Henry and Rog on evaluation use in Chapter Five of this volume).

In this chapter, we discuss social programming from the perspective of emergent realist (ER) evaluation, and we sketch several implications for evaluation practice. The discussion will apply the twin concepts of sensemaking and valuing (which were presented in Chapter Two concerning knowledge construction (Julnes and Mark) and in Chapter Three on valuing (Henry and Julnes)), to the analysis of social programming and policy-making. By considering the nature of social programming and policy-making, this chapter also provides a contextual argument for using the realist approach sketched out in Chapter One of this volume.

We address both policy-making and social programming, though with more explicit attention to the latter. We do not address other evaluands, such as personnel and products, that might be addressed by the transdiscipline of evaluation that Scriven (1993) describes.

Anderson (1990, pp. 5–8) casts the notion of policy-making widely, including (1) the needs or policy demands that are to be addressed, (2) the expression of an intended course of action, (3) the decisions involved in setting that action, (4) the statements that formalize the intentions, and (5) the actions (or inactions) that follow. Shadish, Cook, and Leviton (1991) suggest a different, but similarly broad usage of social programming, which they indicate consists of three elements: (1) the structure and functioning internal to a program; (2) the external constraints that shape and constrain programs; and (3) the processes by which programs change and by which program change contributes to social change. The definitions of social programming and policy-making contain overlapping elements, and there is no clean definition or distinct demarcation between the two. We shall not force a distinction between the two in this chapter, and our discussion generally applies to both.

We do not attempt to provide a comprehensive review of the literatures, theories, or experiences that pertain to social programming. Instead, we will use the concepts of sensemaking and valuing as our point of departure for viewing the world of social programming and for a selective consideration of some of the key characteristics of policies and programs. Following from this, we will consider the roles that ER evaluation can reasonably play in stimulating social change. Although an evaluation theory's model of social programming should have a direct relationship with the intended evaluation use—evaluation prods social change and the ultimate goal of social progress through change in social programs (Henry and Julnes, Chapter Three of this volume)—we will leave the primary discussion of use to Chapter Five (Henry and Rog).

Sensemaking and Valuing in Social Policy-Making and Programming

Although it may serve other purposes, social programming is at least in part an evolved mechanism for dealing with issues that have come to be identified as social problems (Kingdon, 1995). The conditions that are considered social problems are often relatively enduring and difficult ones, such as poverty and crime, which have persisted in the face of previous social problem-solving efforts (Etzioni, 1994). Alternatively, they may be conditions that have been recently created by the unintended consequences of other changes, such as the problem of homeless mentally ill caused by deinstitutionalization (Rog, 1995). In addition, social problems may be enduring conditions that have only recently been defined in a way that warrants organized societal attention. For example, child abuse (Glazer, 1994; Nelson, 1984) and drunk driving (Glazer, 1994) are long-standing social conditions that have recently come to be seen as social problems.

The ER perspective presented in previous chapters provides a framework for viewing social problems. The social conditions that we call social problems are regularized events or outcomes that result from ongoing patterns of social actions and interactions. Social problems arise from underlying generative mechanisms (for example, see Bhaskar, 1978; House, 1991; Pawson and Tilly,

1997). However, different generative mechanisms can give rise to the same social problem. For example, homelessness may result from deinstitutional-ization or from temporary poverty created by males abandoning their families (Wright, 1989). In the case of social conditions such as child abuse, the condition exists independent of our knowledge or recognition of it, but our perception of it changes. For instance, we did not in the past two decades construct physical and mental cruelty to children into *existence*. Rather, we began to construe this cruelty as a medical issue and legitimize it as a target of social concern (Glazer, 1994; Nelson, 1984). But not all undesirable social conditions are construed as social problems. This designation is reserved for those problems for which demands are pressed through the political process and which are legitimized through a social and, in most cases, a governmental process (Anderson, 1990; Kingdon, 1995).

Popper (1994, p. 65), referring both to social and to scientific problems, describes a problem as the conflict between a fact and an expectation. A social problem, then, occurs when a social condition does not meet public expectations for society. Poverty, crime, homelessness, and child abuse are social problems. They are regularly occurring events or conditions that, by the fact of excessive occurrence or by the fact that they happen at all, are problems that have been deemed to require collective action. Social problems require both sensemaking ("facts") and valuing (expectations and judgments of what *should* be).

The ER framework presented in earlier chapters also provides a lens with which to view social programs. Although they may serve other functions, social programs at least in part are organized attempts to address social problems. Social programs can be better understood as social actions and interactions, set in motion by policy, and intended to trigger generative mechanisms to improve conditions. These social actions and interactions are thrust into the existing sets of relationships that produced the original social condition.

Social programming involves sensemaking (see Julnes and Mark, Chapter Two of this volume), where information and beliefs are combined to form an often informal and incomplete understanding of why the problem exists and what can be done about it. Underpinning social programs are judgments about (1) the existence of some problem (Witkin and Altschuld, 1995), (2) possible causes and solutions of the problem (Kingdon, 1995), and (3) mechanisms for delivering services to those experiencing the problem (Scheirer, 1987). These judgments arise from the sensemaking activities of those involved in decisions about social programming. Using a variety of information, from personal anecdotes to systematic studies, these sensemaking activities are often informal and implicit. Researchers in social and political psychology have addressed the cognitive processes through which individuals make judgments about policies and programs, including biases that occur in such judgments (for example, see, Kinder and Sears, 1981).

The policy-making process, then, is from one perspective a sensemaking endeavor that relies on a variety of information sources, including evaluation.

However, values often take center stage in the process of policy-making (White, 1994). Policy deliberations provide a forum for expressing values, whether they emanate from a systematic effort to tap "the national mood" or from the public position of an interested and affected group. Far from being coldly analytical, the process of establishing social problems and programs places us "in the grips of passions, interests, perceptions, and values that are not going to be affected much by what the scientists tell us" (Glazer, 1994, p. 36).

Debates about abortion, welfare, and the criminal justice system, for example, typically reflect deep-seated feelings about right and wrong, about ethics, and about core values that may be relatively resistant to information. To further complicate matters, the primacy with which these values are regarded can change over time, as is the case of welfare reform (Murray, 1984) and child abuse (Nelson, 1984). The values basis of social programs interact, bidirectionally, with the values component of evaluation. Choices made in the evaluation process are influenced by the values in the policy community, and these choices may in turn influence the values that are held and used in the policy debates. For example, evaluations of welfare reform, which have been used in the devolution of welfare programs to the states, have emphasized lowering the welfare rolls and making program recipients work (Gueron, 1997).

In sum, both social programming and evaluation combine sensemaking and value expressive components. In this respect, social programming and evaluation can be seen as parallel endeavors, with very different structures and rules. The sensemaking and valuing aspects of evaluation potentially serve as mechanisms to influence the sensemaking and valuing of the social programming world. Social programming and policy-making are social processes that lead to legitimized collective action. Evaluation, from the emergent realist perspective, seeks to be a part of those social processes, but not, as some early evaluators seemed to hope, to replace them.

Processes that Create and Modify Social Programs

If evaluators aspire to affect the sensemaking and valuing processes of the policy-making and social programming world, then the nature of these processes should be of interest to evaluators. Early in the development of the field of evaluation, there appeared to be a strong belief that these processes were rational, and a corresponding belief in direct instrumental use of evaluation findings in the policy process. However, the reality of these processes is much more complex and interesting. Although no single theory yet adequately explains the processes that underlie the legislative, administrative, and bureaucratic decision-making that creates, constrains, and modifies social programs (see, for example, Lynn, 1994, and Fountain, 1994, for reviews of alternative frameworks), some insights have emerged. And some lessons have been learned that should influence our approach to evaluation.

Psychological and Organizational Complexities. One general lesson concerns the complexity and imperfections in decision-making about social programs. Such decision-making is carried out by humans with imperfect information, limited cognitive abilities, and competing demands, in the context of organizations and situations that may constrain decisions. The perspective of many early evaluators, which implicitly assumed rational decision-making, now appears amazingly naive from several points of view. First, it overestimates the quality, relevance, and comprehensiveness of most evaluations relative to other sources of information. Second, it overestimates the importance of information in the political arena relative to ideology, entrenched interests, and other political concerns. Third, it also assumes a decision-maker is poised to make rational decisions about programs based on the information that evaluations provide. The third assumption has been called into question, for example, by work in cognitive and social psychology that emphasizes the biases and heuristics that influence judgments (for example, see Kahneman, Slovic, and Tversky, 1982). Fourth, it underestimates the impact of organizational and situational processes that constrain decision-making. For example, students of organizations have noted the prevalence of rules based on organizational history, which limit the available decision space (for example, March and Simon, 1958), as well as the extent to which decisions in organizations often emerge, or accrete, over time, rather than being discrete judgments (Weiss, 1988a). Finally, the early evaluation model of policy-making failed to recognize that the policy setting community is often diverse and broader than a few key decision-makers (Cronbach and others, 1980), and that information, including evaluation results, typically does not reach decision-makers directly but is mediated through such mechanisms as staffers, the news media, special-interest groups, and special ("blue ribbon") commissions (Weiss, 1988a).

A second general lesson involves the multidimensional nature of use (Weiss, 1997). Early evaluators expected what has come to be called *direct,* or *instrumental,* use of evaluation results, whereby positive results would lead to the continuation and expansion of effective programs, and negative results to the discontinuation or revision of ineffective programs (Suchman, 1967). The widespread interest that developed in the evaluation community in the early 1980s about the non-utilization of evaluations (see, for example, Weiss and Bucuvalas, 1980) seemed to derive largely from the dashed expectation that evaluation findings would translate directly into decisions about program continuation or revision.

Coinciding with the evaluation community's development of a less naive view of decision-making was an alternative to the view that evaluation use was direct and instrumental. According to this alternative view, evaluation results often serve an educational function (Cronbach, 1982), commonly referred to as "enlightenment" (Weiss, 1977). This conceptual form of utilization can occur, for example, when evaluation results influence the framing of subsequent debates about a social issue, or help inform the design of some new program years after the evaluation. ER evaluators believe that attention to these more conceptual forms of utilization is important, given the imperfections of social decision-making processes that may sometimes act against direct use, and given the desire for evaluations to provide value to individuals other than those identified as intended users when the evaluation is negotiated.

Politics Do Matter. In a discussion of social programming, it goes without saying that politics do matter. Politics matter in creating, constraining, and revising social programs. However, many writers about evaluation have given short shrift to politics, ignoring or minimizing its influence on social programming and evaluation. Weiss (1988b) noted that, in an address focusing on evaluation use, Patton (1988) never once mentioned politics (but see Patton, 1997). Other evaluation theorists have acknowledged the importance of politics in establishing social programs, but have suggested implicitly or explicitly that programs are relatively resistant to change through political means. Similarly, Wholey has emphasized that, if program change is to occur, it should be done internally, by influencing the actions of program managers (for example, see Wholey, 1983).

Before the 1980s, the conventional wisdom in political science and public administration was that political agents (such as the President or Congress) lacked either the ability or the interest to control the bureaucracy that ran social programs (for instance, see Koenig, 1975; Scher, 1960). More recently, empirical research has demonstrated that public bureaucracies are responsive to changes in the political landscape (Wood and Waterman, 1991; Kingdon, 1995). A particularly important mechanism of political control over bureaucracies is through political appointments. Over a considerable array of agencies, the outputs of agencies (often the result of particular programs) were dramatically affected by the entry of new agency administrators (Wood and Waterman, 1991). Kingdon's case studies of health and transportation similarly showed that political appointees were the most influential group inside or outside of government in elevating an issue and sticking to it (1995, pp. 17–30). Other mechanisms, including administrative reorganization, changes in budgets, and legislation, can also make a difference, though typically with less impact than appointments (Wood and Waterman, 1991).

Evidence also exists that more local political activities can influence the operations of bureaucracies. For example, in a study of the enforcement activities of the Occupational Safety and Health Administration, Scholz, Twombly, and Headrick (1991) found that the party affiliation of elected officials was associated with the level of agency enforcement, and that county political parties are more influential for those activities with the most local discretion. That is, local political considerations can influence programs, especially for activities with the most local discretion. This finding is particularly interesting given the increasing devolution of programs, which creates greater flexibility at state and local levels (Pressman and Wildavsky, 1984). Educational policy-making is a case in point, with governors, state legislatures, state boards of education, local school superintendents, local school boards, and principals attempting to constrain the activities of the teacher, who nevertheless operates with wide discretion behind the closed classroom door (Cohen, 1995). This structure produces a wide range of implementation patterns—some of which may be influenced by political considerations—that may in turn affect the program outcomes. This structure also means that there is a wider variety of individuals who may influence the program, beyond direct stakeholders, including attentive and mobilized publics (Rosenau, 1974) and the national mood (Kingdon, 1995). When politics are involved, the public is involved. The role of public and political forces in social programming has implications for ER evaluation, which we address in the final section of this chapter.

The Dynamic Nature of External Forces That Influence Programs

Just as social programs themselves are dynamic, so too are the external forces that create and constrain social programming. In the U.S. experience, the 1960s heralded a fertile period for social programming (Shadish, Cook, and Leviton, 1991). During the 1970s, the lesson seemed to be that social programs never die (Cook, 1981). In the 1980s, however, the so-called Reagan revolution demonstrated that it was possible to curtail, if not kill, programs. And in the 1990s, U.S. budget constraints make it difficult to propose a program without specifying the revenues or other budget cuts that will pay for it. The general concepts of windows of opportunity and honeymoon periods for new administrations also suggest that the political forces that create and constrain social programs vary with time. Similarly, the findings of Wood and Waterman (1991) suggest that the conservative and rule-bound nature of organizations described by organizational theorists such as March and Simon (1958) are subject to periodic upheaval in the political arena, with nonlinear, dynamic change. Neither rational nor simply incremental, the process of policy change appears to be the conjunction of three independent streams: social problems, alternative solutions, and politics (Kingdon, 1995).

Dynamic change in social programs does not have to involve broad societal forces. For example, Weiss (1988b) describes a case in which an evaluation found evidence of modest program success, and it made several recommendations for improvements. As the evaluation ended, a new head of the parent agency was appointed, and he did not have a high priority for this program (compare to Wood and Waterman, 1991; Kingdon 1995). In Weiss' (1988b) words: "The director of the program was encouraged to leave, and the program was relegated to peripheral status in the agency. All the evidence of success and important recommendations found their way into professional publications, from whence they may rise someday to affect the next reincarnation of the program." Most experienced evaluators have similar stories, in which the potential of direct utilization was dashed by the disappearance of key players or the changing of agency or legislative priorities. Of course, some evaluators have the reverse kind of story to tell, in which all of the stars in the constellations came into alignment, and direct utilization followed. Either way, policy windows often open and close with little regard to whether and when evaluations are available.

We should not be surprised by the dynamic nature of the forces that influence programs. To the contrary, change in the social organizations that create and modify social programs is virtually inevitable— but not necessarily highly predictable—given the potential for change in the forces that impact these organizations (such as the political party in power). Moreover, this type of change is consistent with many realists' discussions of organic processes, dynamic change, and open systems in social systems (for example, see Bhaskar, 1978; Popper, 1957). The dynamic nature of change in the factors that shape social programs has implications for ER evaluation, which we will consider in the final section of this chapter.

The Internal Structure and Functioning of Programs

Program theorists (for example, Bickman, 1990; Chen, 1990) have provided the most cogent arguments for evaluators to concern themselves with questions about the internal structure of programs. Program theorists emphasize the need to know more about how programs work for evaluation to contribute to program improvement. Emergent realist evaluation endorses this perspective and further specifies that program theory should (1) emphasize variation in implementation, (2) attend to the mechanisms that underlie the linkage between program activities and outcomes, and (3) assess (a) whether different mechanisms operate under different conditions, and (b) whether the program and its various elements have different effects for different types of participants under different circumstances, all while (4) evaluators should also recognize that these sensemaking activities are best accompanied by systematic inquiry and critical examination of values. We turn now to three salient aspects of the internal structure and functioning of social programs: implementation, the robustness of programs, and the contingent causality of program effects.

The Importance of Implementation. Because they recognize the complexities of social programs operating in an open system, ER evaluators are concerned with implementation. In early evaluations, it was implicitly assumed that interventions were implemented in a relatively homogeneous and meaningful fashion. Among the sins that resulted were (1) aggregating projects that provided vastly different services because they bore a common program name, (2) evaluating programs that had not actually been implemented or had been implemented inadequately, and (3) being unable to identify the specific programmatic actions (or inactions) that led to success or failure.

Evaluators subsequently came to recognize that (1) services may be delivered in very different ways under the auspices of a single program; (2) program staff may adapt service delivery, for a variety of reasons, relative to the stated characteristics of a program; (3) programs are often defined in general ways, with important decisions left up to the street-level service deliverer. Consequently, evaluation theorists have presented detailed procedures for assessing the characteristics of programs as designed and implemented, under labels such as evaluability assessment (Wholey, 1983), implementation assessment (Scheirer, 1987), and program theory (Bickman, 1990; Chen, 1990). For similar reasons, the study of implementation, program variation, and context is an important task for ER evaluation.

Robustness of Intervention. Although most social programs are subject to change and adaptations in the implementation process, this may not be (equally) true in all cases. Some interventions are relatively robust in terms of how they are implemented. The most obvious examples, like Social Security in the United States, involve transfers of money. Similarly, the subsidizing of college attendance through changes in the tax code is far more robust in its delivery than is the typical educational intervention, where the program must be carried out by classroom teachers who vary in their commitment and ability and who are likely to adapt the program to their particular context.

Robustness, in the statistical literature, refers to resistance to violations of assumptions that are necessary to yield unbiased estimates or to test hypothesis. When applied to programs, we can make a distinction between robustness with respect to implementation, on the one hand, and robustness with respect to mechanisms and effects, on the other. A program may be robust with respect to implementation but not robust with respect to mechanisms and effects. For example, the new federal higher education financial assistance program, known as the HOPE scholarship, is robust with respect to implementation of the components of the program. Being administered through the tax code constrains local variation. However, the program may vary, across individuals and contexts, in the mechanisms that it triggers and in the effects that it has. For example, the HOPE scholarship program may have less effect on students who are deciding *whether* they will go to college than on those who are considering *where* they will attend (Hossler, Braxton, and Coppersmith, 1989). This and other differences in outcome, and in apparent underlying mechanisms, have been observed in evaluations of the Georgia program on which the federal program was modeled (Davis, Hall, and Henry, 1995; Henry and Bugler, 1996).

Contingent Causality in Social Programs. From the emergent realist perspective, if social programs have effects, it is because they serve as triggers, setting in motion a causal sequence of events based on underlying generative mechanisms. However, these mechanisms may not operate in all cases, or may be balanced out by countervailing forces. As a result, ER evaluators attend closely to whether program effects vary across types of individuals, social settings, and outcomes. These specifications reflect the contingent nature of causality and depart from the notion of constant conjunction that underpins much of the literature on causality dating back to Hume (to understand the importance of this departure, see House, 1991; and Julnes and Mark, Chapter Two of this volume).

Mackie (1965, 1974) provides a useful conceptualization of the contingent nature of causality, which Cronbach (1982), House (1991), and others have imported into the program evaluation literature. We also rely on it for ER evaluation.

Mackie suggests that what we think of as causes are actually "INUS conditions," that is, an Insufficient but Necessary part of a condition which is itself Unnecessary but Sufficient to cause the result. For example, a dropped cigarette may be identified as the cause of a house fire. It is insufficient, by itself, in that other conditions also had to occur, such as the presence of combustible material and the absence of a sprinkler system. But the cigarette was a necessary component of the specific and actual causal package that caused the fire—the fire would not have started spontaneously. The causal package that included the dropped cigarette was unnecessary in that there are several other causal packages that could have led to a fire (for instance, an electrical short circuit). But the package of conditions including the cigarette was sufficient to cause the house fire. The logic of INUS causes can be readily applied to social programs, as the discussion of boot camps in Chapter One of this sourcebook shows.

Social Programming and the Practice of Emergent Realist Evaluation

We can summarize the preceding selective review of social programming as follows. Social programming is at least in part an evolved mechanism for dealing with issues that have come to be identified as social problems. Evaluation can contribute to the sensemaking and valuing that underlies social programming and policy-making. The processes that create and modify social programs involve imperfect decision-making in the midst of organizational and psychological constraints. Use of evaluation findings—or of other information—is multidimensional and can range from direct instrumental use to enlightenment. Politics matter in social programming, including in the modification of social programs, whether through such mechanisms as political appointments or through less-well-understood influences of local political forces on local implementation. Forces that influence social programs are dynamic, with windows of opportunity opening and closing in often unpredictable ways that pay little regard to evaluation timetables. With respect to the internal structure of programs, implementation is critically important and, although some programs may be relatively robust with respect to implementation, most are not. Further, even programs that are robust with respect to how they are implemented may be quite variable in terms of the mechanisms they trigger and the effects they have on different persons and in different contexts. And the mechanisms that are triggered by social programs will usually not have inevitable, uniform effects. Instead, whether effects occur, and how large they are, depends on the presence or absence of other ingredients from the causal package required for the mechanism to be effective. From this selective review of social programming and policy-making, we can draw several implications for ER evaluation.

The Importance of Planning for Enlightenment. Several aspects of the policy-making and social programming process suggest that evaluators should not restrict themselves to seeking direct, instrumental use, but should plan for findings that may facilitate enlightenment. First, the complex and imperfect forms of decision-making that characterize the social programming process may sometimes act against instrumental use. Second, contrary to common conventional wisdom of the past, program personnel are not the only route to influencing program activities, even for established programs. Thus, an enlightenment function that serves a broad political audience, including the public, may create long-term effects for evaluations. Third, as evaluators should know, dynamic changes may occur that alter the susceptibility of social programming to evaluation findings, for example, as the result of a change in political parties. Evaluators who narrowly plan for direct use by specific groups of change agents risk delivering an answer to a question no one is interested in by the end of the evaluation. Further, by adding to the explanatory base of knowledge, evaluators can influence future decisions and decisions in other settings, as well as inform immediate decisions.

Of course, planning for enlightenment use does not imply that one should eschew the possibility of direct, instrumental use. To the contrary, in the course of ER evaluation one should attempt, within the limits of evaluation resources, to both probe underlying mechanisms to facilitate enlightenment, and provide specific guidance about possible program improvements to facilitate direct use. Moreover, as discussed in Chapter One in this volume, the evaluation work done to facilitate enlightenment (probing underlying generative mechanisms and studying values) should also lead to direct use in many cases.

Studying *Why* What Works for Whom. If ER evaluation seeks to facilitate enlightenment, how does it attempt to do so? In looking for more useful approaches to evaluation, but not from an ER perspective, many scholars have noted the value of addressing the question, What works for whom under what conditions? In a review of the evaluation of educational reform, Corcoran and Goertz (1995, p. 29) posed the problem this way: "Our knowledge about what works under different conditions with different types of students is limited." Similarly, in her evaluation of early childhood programs, Marcon states, ". . .we could no longer assume that just any preschool curriculum will achieve positive results. We need to identify effective matches between curriculum and child characteristics" (1994, p. 8). In a review of the evaluations in the field of criminal justice, Pawson and Tilley (1997) find a need to specify the conditions under which particular outcomes are achieved and to focus on the nature of the intervention that works to reduce types of crimes committed by particular types of offenders. These and other authors define a strikingly similar need across very different fields of social programming—the need to peer underneath the net effect and to achieve a finer-grained understanding of what works for whom under what conditions. This focus can be more fully specified: *what*—which program services delivered how; *works*—influences diverse outcomes valued by different stakeholders and the public; *for whom*—with which types of the diverse individuals that programs serve; *under what circumstances*—in which of the contexts in which the program operates?

Addressing this question provides information that can be used for enlightenment purposes. However, from the ER perspective, it is generally more desirable to address the "What works" question from the context of studying the underlying generative mechanisms: Why is it that some aspects of the program may affect specific outcomes, for particular types of clients, under particular conditions? An account based on mechanisms, on why things work, is more likely to provide a psychologically satisfactory and memorable account (Einhorn and Hogarth, 1986), and thus to enter into the indirect and mediated chain of events (Weiss, 1988b) that leads to enlightenment. Moreover, having an explanation is likely to increase one's confidence about the validity and plausibility of generalizing from past findings (Cronbach, 1982; Mark, 1994). Numerous other evaluators and evaluation theorists have also emphasized the importance of trying to develop substantive knowledge or theory from evaluations (for example, Cronbach, 1982).

The "What works" question can also be viewed from the perspective of contingent causality as described by Mackie. From this perspective, one of the most important ER evaluation tasks is to identify the elements of the causal package to which the program belongs (see Chapters One and Two regarding methods for this task and that of probing mechanisms).

Studying What Works—the Importance of Assessing Implementation. Several aspects of our review of selected key characteristics of social programming lead to the conclusion that it is important for ER evaluation to attend closely to how programs are implemented. First, considerable literature indicates that in most programs, implementation varies across sites. Second, implementation may be influenced by politics (and other contextual factors). And third, differences in implementation, that is, in the specific services offered, can lead to differences in what, if any, underlying mechanisms are triggered. Program services act as the trigger in the sequence of causally related events through which programs have their effects. It is important to know which program attributes generate which specific outcomes. Consequently, evaluators should develop and test plausible models about the specific services that trigger causal mechanisms and result in particular outcomes.

Molar and Molecular Perspectives on Program Effects. The distinction between molar and molecular perspectives is important in ER evaluation (see Chapters One and Two). For example, for a preschool program for four-year-olds, the molar question might simply be, Does the program produce long-term cognitive gains for participants? In contrast, a more molecular analysis might ask, What are the differential impacts of different preschool teachers' practices, such as child-initiated versus teacher-directed instruction, on reducing retention in the first grade for disadvantaged versus advantaged students, and by what mechanisms do they occur (Marcon, 1994)?

Several aspects of our review of social programming support the importance of considering molar and molecular perspectives. First, variation in implementation is commonplace and may be the result of political or other contextual forces. The diversity of influences on social programs, along with the local discretion that characterizes most social programs, leads to a complex array of services and methods of service delivery. Second, the contingent view of causality suggests that these local variations are likely to matter, as discussed previously. And third, the structure of social programming itself typically varies along a molar versus molecular dimension, ranging from more centralized entities such as Congress or a state governor, to more localized entities such as the individual service recipient. Indeed, the structure of social programming can produce a challenge for evaluators: National (or state, in the case of state-based programs) policy-makers who fund the evaluation may be more interested in the molar question (Does the program, overall, work?) whereas those at local levels are more interested in more molecular questions, (Does it work here, at my site, or with my child?).

Based on our picture of social programming and on ER principles presented in previous chapters, we offer five comments about molar versus molecular analyses. First, judgments about the level of the audience for evaluation findings, as well as the relative likelihood and importance in a particular instance of enlightenment versus direct utilization, may move the evaluator to a decision about whether to emphasize molar or molecular analyses. Second, more informed molecular analyses are possible to the extent that we have good theories that specify the expected pattern of differences across types of clients, settings, and treatment variations. An ER evaluator is likely to begin with more molar analyses to the extent that good theory is lacking. Third, as described in Chapters One and Two, more molar investigations should be joined with more exploratory analyses aimed at discovering (and, to the extent possible, independently confirming) more molecular understanding. Fourth, to the extent it is *practical*, we prefer molecular to molar accounts. In general, programs vary too much, serve individuals that are too diverse, and operate in contexts that are too different for global statements of effectiveness to be deeply meaningful. Estimates of the overall mean effect of programs, while they may be accurately assessed, may miss important patterns of observable variation. For instance, some programs may work well to increase the educational attainment of African-American children, but not of Hispanic-Americans. Unless evaluation approaches take these potential variations into account, they may fail to contribute to the understanding of the program and to improving social conditions. But, fifth, this is not to say that a molar examination of program effects is never appropriate or useful. In fact, it can be very useful, for instance, in establishing a social problem as important and legitimate (see Henry and Rog, Chapter Five in this volume). Again, however, as a general rule, a molar approach should be joined with attempts at principled discovery (see Chapters One and Two) to move toward more molecular understanding.

Inquiry into Values, as Well as Sensemaking. Thus far, the implications we have drawn from our analysis of social programming and policy-making focus on sensemaking, with special emphasis on testing explanatory accounts of program effects, assessing the nature and consequences of variations in program implementation, and asking, What works for whom under what conditions, and why? A final implication we will draw from our selective review of social programming is the appropriateness, in ER evaluation, of empirically studying and critically examining values. The very process of defining a condition as a social problem worthy of collective action involves valuing as well as sensemaking. Similarly, the processes through which social programs are created and revised involve valuing as well as sensemaking. In addition, the values of the social programming world influence evaluation, for example, in the selection of outcome measures, and the values of evaluations can likewise influence the social programming world.

In short, a review of several key characteristics of social programming and policy-making supports many of the attributes of emergent realist evaluation presented throughout this volume, including its emphasis on the dual tasks of sensemaking and valuing, the importance of seeking enlightenment use through the study of underlying generative mechanisms, the value of the molar versus molecular distinction, and the utility of studying variations in implementation and assessing what works for whom in what circumstances.

References

Anderson, J. E. *Public Policymaking.* Boston: Houghton Mifflin, 1990.

Bhaskar, R. A. *A Realist Theory of Science.* Atlantic Highlands, N.J.: Humanities Press, 1978.

Bickman, L. (ed.). *Advances in Program Theory.* New Directions for Program Evaluation, no. 47. San Francisco: Jossey-Bass, 1990.

Chen, H.-t. *Theory-Driven Evaluations.* Newbury Park, Calif.: Sage, 1990.

Cohen, D. K. "Standards-Based School Reform: Policy, Practice, and Performance." Paper presented at the Brooks Conference on Performance-Based Approaches to School Reform, Washington, D.C., 1995.

Cook, T. D. "Dilemmas in the Evaluation of Social Programs." In M. B. Brewer and B. E. Collins (eds.), *Scientific Inquiry and the Social Sciences: A Volume in Honor of Donald T. Campbell.* San Francisco: Jossey-Bass, 1981.

Corcoran, D., and Goertz, M. "Institutional Capacity and High-Performance Schools." *Educational Researcher,* 1995, 24 (9), 27–31.

Cronbach, L. J. *Designing Evaluations of Educational and Social Programs.* San Francisco: Jossey-Bass, 1982.

Cronbach, L. J., and others. *Toward Reform of Program Evaluation.* San Francisco: Jossey-Bass, 1980.

Davis, M., Hall, T., and Henry, G. *Report on the Expenditure of Lottery Funds, Fiscal Year 1995.* Atlanta, Ga.: Council for School Performance, 1995.

Einhorn, H. J., and Hogarth, R. M. "Judging Probable Cause." *Psychological Bulletin,* 1986, 99, 3–19.

Etzioni, A. "Incorrigible." *The Atlantic Monthly,* July 1, 1994, 74, pp. 14, 16.

Fountain, J. E. "Comment: Disciplining Public Management Research." *Journal of Policy Analysis and Management,* 1994, 13 (2), 269–277.

Glazer, N. "How Social Problems are Born." *The Public Interest,* 1994, 115, 31–44.

Gueron, J. M. "Learning About Welfare Reform: Lessons from State-Based Evaluations." In D. J. Rog and D. Fournier (eds.), *Progress and Future Directions in Evaluations: Perspectives on Theory, Practice, and Methods.* New Directions for Evaluation, no. 76. San Francisco: Jossey-Bass, 1997.

Henry, G., and Bugler, D. *Evaluation of the HOPE Scholarship Program.* Atlanta, Ga.: Council for School Performance, 1996.

Hossler, D., Braxton, J., and Coppersmith, G. "Understanding Student College Choice." In J. Smart (ed.) *Higher Education: Handbook of Theory and Research.* New York: Agathon Press, 1989.

House, E. R. "Realism in Research." *Educational Researcher,* 1991, *20,* 2–9.

Kahneman, D., Slovic, P., and Tversky, A. (eds.). *Judgment Under Uncertainty: Heuristics and Biases.* New York: Cambridge University Press, 1982.

Kinder, D. R., and Sears, D. O. "Prejudice and Politics: Symbolic Racism Versus Racial Threats to the Good Life." *Journal of Personality and Social Psychology,* 1981, *40,* 414–431.

Kingdon, J. *Agendas, Alternatives, and Public Policies.* (2nd ed.) Boston: HarperCollins, 1995.

Koenig, L. W. *The Chief Executive.* New York: Harcourt, Brace, 1975.

Lynn, L. E., Jr. "Public Management Research: The Triumph of Art over Science." *Journal of Policy Analysis and Management,* 1994, *13* (2), 231–259.

Mackie, J. L. "Causes and Conditions." *American Philosophical Quarterly,* 1965, 2 (4), 245–255, 261–264.

Mackie, J. L. *The Cement of the Universe: A Study of Causation.* Oxford: Clarendon, 1974.

March, J. G,. and Simon, H. A. *Organizations.* New York: Wiley, 1958.

Marcon, R. "Doing the Right Thing for Children: Linking Research and Policy Reform in the District of Columbia Public Schools." *Young Children,* 1994, 2–10.

Mark, M. M. "Validity Typologies and the Logic and Practice of Quasi-Experimentation." In W.M.K. Trochim (ed.), *Advances in Quasi-Experimental Design and Analysis.* New Directions for Program Evaluation, no. 31. San Francisco: Jossey-Bass, 1994.

Murray, C. *Losing Ground: American Social Policy 1950–1980. New York: Basic Books,* 1984.

Nelson, B. J. *Making an Issue of Child Abuse.* Chicago: University of Chicago Press, 1984.

Patton, M. Q. "The Evaluator's Responsibility for Utilization." *Evaluation Practice,* 1988, *9,* 5–24.

Patton, M. Q. *Utilization-Focused Evaluation.* (3rd ed.) Thousand Oaks, Calif.: Sage, 1997.

Pawson, R., and Tilly, N. *Realistic Evaluation.* Thousand Oaks, Calif.: Sage, 1997.

Popper, K. *The Poverty of Historicism.* London: Routledge, 1957.

Popper, K. *In Search of a Better World.* New York: Routledge, 1994.

Pressman, J. L., and Wildavsky, A. *Implementation.* (3rd ed.) Berkeley: University of California Press, 1984.

Rosenau, J. *Citizenship Between Elections: An Inquiry into the Mobilizable American.* Macmillan, 1974.

Scheirer, M. A. "Program Theory and Implementation Theory: Implications for Evaluators." In L. Bickman (ed.), *Using Program Theory in Evaluation.* New Directions for Program Evaluation, no. 33. San Francisco: Jossey-Bass, 1987.

Scher, S. "Congressional Committee Members as Independent Agency Overseers: A Case Study." *American Political Science Review,* 1960, *54,* 911–20.

Scholz, J. T., Twombly, J., and Headrick, B. "Street-Level Political Controls over Federal Bureaucracy." *American Political Science Review,* 1991, *85* (3), 829–850.

Scriven, M. S. *Hard-Won Lessons in Program Evaluation.* New Directions for Program Evaluation, no. 58. San Francisco: Jossey-Bass, 1993.

Shadish, W. R., Cook, T. D., and Leviton, L. C. *Foundations of Program Evaluation: Theories of Practice.* Newbury Park, Calif.: Sage, 1991.

Suchman, E. A. *Evaluative Research: Principles and Practice in Public Service and Social Action Programs.* New York: Russell Sage Foundation, 1967.

Weiss, C. H. "Do We Know Any More About Evaluation Use?" Plenary address at annual meeting of the American Evaluation Association, San Diego, Calif., 1997.

Weiss, C. H. "If Program Decisions Hinged Only on Information: A Response to Patton." *Evaluation Practice,* 1988b, *9,* 15–28.

Weiss, C. H. "Evaluation for Decisions: Is Anybody There? Does Anybody Care?" *Evaluation Practice,* 1988a, *9,* 5–20.

Weiss, C. H. "Research for Policy's Sake: The Enlightenment Function of Social Research." *Policy Analysis,* 1977, *3,* 531–545.

Weiss, C. H., and Bucuvalas, M. J. *Social Science Research and Decision-Making.* New York: Columbia University Press, 1980.

White, L. "Policy Analysis as Discourse." *Journal of Policy Analysis and Management,* 1994, *13* (3), 506–525.

Wholey, J. S. *Evaluation and Effective Public Management.* Boston: Little, Brown, 1983.

Witkin, B. R., and Altschuld, J. W. *Planning and Conducting Needs Assessments: A Practical Guide.* Thousand Oaks, Calif.: Sage, 1995.

Wood, B. D., and Waterman, R. W. "The Dynamics of Political Control of the Bureaucracy." *American Political Science Review,* 1991, *85* (3), 801–828.

Wright, J. D. *Address Unknown: The Homeless in America.* New York: A. de Gruyter, 1989.

A theory of evaluation use must be contextualized within the venue in which use is expected. Use in policy-making and social programming is analyzed with particular emphasis on shaping realist practice to increase the potential for utilization.

A Realist Theory and Analysis of Utilization

Gary T. Henry, Debra J. Rog*

Since the 1970s, evaluation theorists have struggled with the recognition that evaluation findings often have little influence on policy decision-making. The role of evaluation within a pluralist democracy was given considerable scrutiny by theorists and the growing contingent of evaluation scholars (for example, see Weiss, 1972, 1973, 1977) as ideas about use moved from idealism to empiricism. For our perspective on uses of evaluation, we turn the emergent realist (ER) lens toward the process of social policy-making and programming to offer ways that evaluation can affect utilization. Once again, the twin processes of sensemaking and valuing are the keys to our theory and analysis of evaluation utilization.

The realist view of utilization begins by recognizing that the processes of sensemaking and valuing are different and distinct between the communities of policy-making and social programming, and those of evaluation and research (Dunn, 1980; Wingens, 1990). For an evaluation to be utilized, the evaluation must be designed, implemented, analyzed, and reported in ways that are sensitive to the different processes that operate in the world of social policy-making and programming.

In an ER evaluation, we are interested in understanding the generative mechanisms that underlie utilization, much as we are in understanding the mechanisms that underlie social programs and policies. In Chapter Four on social programming, Mark and Henry emphasize the characteristics of the processes that affect how evaluations are conducted. In this chapter, we discuss the factors and processes that affect whether and how evaluation findings are used. We base the emergent realist theory of utilization in the best existing theory and knowledge on the utilization of evaluation and research findings.

*DEBRA J. ROG is a research fellow at the Vanderbilt University Institute for Public Policy Studies, where she directs the Washington office of the Center for Mental Health Policy.

In so doing, this analysis allows for an integrative understanding of how use is triggered by aspects of the evaluation itself, the specific policy context, the specific stage of the policy process, the stakeholders involved, and so forth. The emergent realist perspective on utilization, therefore, acknowledges that, much like our evaluations attempt to understand What works for whom under what conditions?, our quest here is to understand What types of evaluations are useful for what audiences under what policy conditions?

We begin by defining what we mean by utilization in ERE. After defining use, we bring to bear Kingdon's description of policy-making, and we use the four stages in his framework to organize the remainder of the chapter.

Defining Utilization

In a comprehensive review of the literature on evaluation utilization, Schula and Cousins (1997) find that most reviews of utilization literature have produced a tripartite conceptualization. The three similar types of use are (1) instrumental use, or the direct use of results in making decisions about programs; (2) enlightenment, or the use of findings to influence the way a program or its effects are viewed; (3) symbolic or persuasive use of evaluation findings to retrospectively support a decision made prior to the evaluation finding. In essence, utilization conceptualized in these terms accepts evaluation as the defining social process for understanding use. Weiss has been the strongest proponent of an alternative way of viewing utilization (1988), suggesting that the pluralist values and complex processes of social decision-making become the context for a theory of utilization.

In this chapter, utilization is contextualized within the policy process. Wingens (1990) has suggested that the social systems operating within the evaluation and policy-making arenas can be quite different. Both have rather well-evolved means of sensemaking and valuing (see Mark and Henry, Chapter Four). Therefore, to understand utilization, it is first important to analyze the social policy system, differentiate its stages, and address the types and uses of information within each stage. From an ER perspective, within the policy process, the object of inquiry is to determine how evaluation processes and findings can trigger a generative mechanism that results in use of evaluation findings.

The best received theory of the policy process (Kingdon 1995, pp. 2–3) sets out four stages, or components, for policy-making and social programming:

1. Setting the agenda
2. Specifying alternatives from which choice is to be made
3. Making an authoritative choice among those specified alternatives, as in a legislative vote or a presidential decision
4. Implementing the decision

Often evaluation is considered a separate stage following implementation. On the contrary, we see the strong potential for evaluation to be conducted during and to influence all stages. Evaluation is not a separate stage, but a parallel process that can brought to bear at any point in the policy process. In fact, Kingdon's work suggests that these four subprocesses are less aptly described as sequential and more accurately positioned as four overlapping streams of activity. By distinguishing forms of utilization that are tied to each of these stages in the policy-making process, the ER perspective offers an opportunity for developing a contextual understanding of utilization by revealing the generative mechanisms that different types of evaluation findings may trigger.

Setting the Policy Agenda

Setting the agenda begins with reframing a social condition as a social problem through collective definition (Hilgartner and Bosk, 1988). Problems can rise to the agenda through significant singular events (such as, disasters), or through series of events (such as, riots or protests); through the gradual accumulation of knowledge; through changes in technology; or through persistent prodding by advocates and others (Davidson and Oleszek, 1985). As Mark and Henry explain in Chapter Four, neither the magnitude of the problem nor deteriorating conditions determine whether the problem appears on the policy agenda. Similarly, conditions that appear to be improving do not lessen public concern with some issues: witness the decrease in violent crime yet the continued fear of crime.

Defining social problems involves a competition in which social conditions are contrasted with societal expectations for a place on the governmental agenda and the attention and resources that follow (Hilgartner and Bosk, 1988). Within this arena, evaluators are one among many groups—such as politicians, reporters, interest groups, political appointees, civil servants, "the public opinion," and campaign operatives—vying to get issues raised and acted on (Kingdon, 1995; Glazer, 1994; Portz, 1996; Hilgartner and Bosk, 1988). Under what conditions can evaluations trigger a set of events that lead to placing a social problem on the government agenda?

First, evaluations can produce the evidence to establish that a legitimate problem exists. This sensemaking capacity of evaluation, along with a perception of the independence of evaluators and the weight of empirically based knowledge, undergirds the potential social impact of the information produced by evaluators. Evaluations can produce findings that describe the magnitude or severity of a problem, its incidence or prevalence, the results of past efforts to ameliorate it, gaps in knowledge of the problem, and the problem's novelty (Chelimsky, 1991; Rochefort and Cobb, 1984). For example, evaluators have produced information on the rates of teenage pregnancies, the extent of mental illness among persons who are homeless, and the fluctuation of welfare receipt for most people receiving welfare.

Even when an evaluation is intended to focus on examining the implementation and/or outcomes of a particular program, the evaluation may promote greater utilization if data can extend beyond examining the program to provide insight into the social conditions that the program confronts. For example, in a recent nine-site evaluation of a program for homeless families (Rog and others, 1995), a large focus of the evaluation was on understanding the needs and characteristics of the families in addition to understanding the outcomes of the program and its implementation. Providing detailed family-level information helped to frame the problem and, in so doing, the possible range of actions for both practitioners and policy-makers.

Other characteristics that affect whether a problem will receive attention in the policy-making arena include drama, severity, novelty or saturation, and culture and politics (Hilgartner and Bosk, 1988). The dramatic impact of extreme findings can raise the visibility of an issue substantially and contribute to the use of an evaluation in agenda setting. In the 1980s, for example, knowledge of the exceptional health needs of homeless individuals (for example, their rate of tuberculosis is 100 times that of the general population) led to greater recognition of the need for increased health care access for individuals living on the streets and in shelters (Wright, 1991).

Novel findings also are likely to gain more attention from the media and others and thus enhance the chance to appear on the agenda for policy-making. A performance monitoring report on schools in Georgia focused on chronic absenteeism (defined as the percentage of students missing ten or more days of school per year), rather than the more usual indicator, attendance. It was a novel presentation of common data and was picked up by the media and frequently discussed in legislative hearings and by school boards and administrators. The novelty of framing the problem as chronic absenteeism rather than as the more usual attendance catapulted the problem into the policy agenda. Problems that cease being novel often fade from the agenda until they are reframed.

The alignment of an issue with both cultural and political values also provides competitive advantage for space in the policy arena. For example, school attendance is a well-seated cultural value, and education is at the top of most lists of public concerns (see for example, Elam, Rose, and Gallup, 1996). The Georgia evaluation also related chronic absenteeism to lower test scores and higher drop-out rates, both of which are widely shared concerns in the political and cultural spheres.

Finally, whether an evaluation finding actually brings a problem onto the agenda depends partly on timing. The policy agenda is notably less crowded at some times, and greater opportunities may be available for issues to emerge on the agenda on these occasions.

Therefore, in the agenda-setting stage of policy making, an evaluation is used when it triggers events that lead to the placing of an issue on the agenda as a social problem. This differs from other conceptions of direct use, in that no instrumental action is taken, no decision is made. However, it is not as diffuse as the general notion of enlightenment. It has a flavor of the utilization of findings as persuasion, but it is also distinct from that and more specific. Neither is this a normative perspective, for one cannot say that the problem that ascends to the agenda is the most important or deserving of attention. If the evaluation is accurate, the status of the conditions is reported in a way that allows participants in the process to assess the importance of the conditions by contrasting the conditions with their expectations.

Specifying Policy Alternatives

The specification of alternatives is an independent stage of the policy-making process, sometimes referred to as policy formulation. It is independent because often policy alternatives are posed for problems that have yet to appear on the public agenda. In fact, as Kingdon found, many solutions require a substantial gestation period during which the policy community and the public are made ready for the alternative, or "softened up," while the ideas mature (1995, p. 128). The need to work out the bugs in a solution often presents opportunities to evaluate pilot programs, but this hinders instrumental use in a finite time period. In many ways it seems that some varieties of formative evaluation and policy analysis jointly refine the solution and soften up the community responsible for accepting it (Patton 1988, 1996).

Alternative solutions are frequently linked to a framing of the social problem. In fact, the way social problems are defined often limits the alternatives that are potential responses to a problem. When homelessness was defined primarily as a problem for persons with mental illness, alternatives to the problem focused on treatment approaches, rather than housing and employment approaches. Evaluations and evaluators can be influential in the winnowing of solutions from the list of proposed alternatives, but the generative mechanism for doing that is quite distinct from the way evaluations may trigger agenda-setting use.

Once again, we can use the sensemaking and valuing aspects of policy-making to predict the ways an evaluation can trigger a series of events that will lead to its use in formulating policy alternatives. From the sensemaking standpoint, alternatives must be technically feasible and within reasonable cost parameters (Kingdon, 1995). Concerns include whether the various solutions can work within economic and political realities. Legislators and their committees, bureaucrats, and experts in the substantive area use their experiential knowledge base to critique alternatives. These professionals and public officials form issue networks within which problems and solutions churn (Heclo, 1978). Evaluators can be among the issues networks, but frequently they are not. Rather, evaluators are in the position of trying to inform and influence these networks with evaluation findings.

In light of evaluation's possible use in the selection of alternatives, some practical design considerations can be identified for emergent realist evaluation. First, ER evaluation concentrates on identifying the generative mechanisms in a program or policy that result in specific outcomes. The most touted evaluation design in some circles is the "true" experiment. While randomized experiments *can* be used within the emergent realist framework, random assignment is not the highest-order value for an ER evaluation. Randomized experiments can *permit* a black box approach to estimate the effect size with little attention to the processes in operation (Lipsey, 1993). This statement is often misread to imply that randomized experiments *must* be conducted in a manner that relegates process variables into a black box, as we see in Majone (1989). A randomized experimental design can include the specification and measurement of process variables that are expected to trigger the generative mechanisms for the outcomes and those that trigger any plausible rival explanations of the outcomes. The theory-driven approach to evaluation (see Weiss, 1997) has been a major push in this direction.

An ER randomized experiment would investigate the possible mechanisms that lead to outcomes, beginning with the triggers for each. See, for example, the mechanisms described for the pre-proposal in Mark, Henry, and Julnes, Chapter One of this volume. For an ER experiment, these mechanisms would be included in the study design so that the way individuals are affected by the program can be understood, recognizing that different individuals may benefit from various combinations of these mechanisms. This is a powerful means of providing information that could be useful in narrowing the range of alternatives under consideration.

The ER evaluation perspective is not unique in eschewing the black box approach to evaluation or in making a call (or cry in the wilderness) for an approach that joins theory with methods (Lipsey, 1993; 1997). But in addition to increasing the strength of the conclusion that a mechanism produced the outcome, this theory-based approach increases the generalizability of the findings. Specifying causal mechanisms offers a means to extrapolate findings beyond an individual evaluation (as well as to begin to accumulate knowledge, rather than simply produce multiple evaluations) by using explanation (Mark, 1986). This is especially important for selecting alternatives, since it requires extrapolating findings from sites where the alternatives have been tried to other sites, a process more akin to argumentation than demonstration (Majone, 1989, pp. 22–23).

In addition to the sensemaking capacity of evaluation, the extent to which the evaluation incorporates various sets of values can be expected to affect the ability of the findings to trigger events, leading to subsequent use of the findings in selecting policy alternatives. The first set of values within the policy community are those held by the specialists within the particular arena. Equity, distribution of benefits, administrative burden, and effectiveness can be key considerations of these stakeholders. In addition to the policy specialists' values, Kingdon mentions two types of value concerns that are present in the selection of alternative solutions: cost and public acquiescence (1995, p. 138). Cost data alone may not lead to clear understanding of which alternatives to select. More costly solutions may or may not be more effective, but cost issues are often raised in current evaluations.

The issue of public opinion has received much less attention (see Henry and Julnes, Chapter Three) than that of specialists' values. ER evaluation opens up the definition of stakeholder to include the public, and in so doing, enhances the likelihood that the evaluation can be used in this stage because of the importance of public opinion in sifting through potential alternatives. The recommendations for solutions that are generated by an evaluation can be tested for public acquiescence or consensus through public opinion polls (Henry, 1996). In addition, surveys and focus groups can reveal the values, concerns, and issues of the public standing in discussions of policy alternatives, rather than have others, armed only with anecdotal information, speak for the public. Evaluations that include information on public opinion may be better able to meet the criticism that their recommendations are out of sync with public sentiment.

As observers have pointed out, the "instrumental rationality" of evaluation use evokes the metaphor of evaluation as demonstration (Majone, 1989). However, evaluation's potential for argument (Campbell, 1982) rather than demonstration is more likely to trigger its use in selecting among an array of potential alternatives. The argumentation metaphor stresses the importance of criticism in the growth of knowledge (Popper, 1994). The likelihood that an evaluation will be used for arguing the strengths and deficiencies of various alternatives is enhanced in several circumstances: when the findings speak to the specific features of a program that cause specific outcomes for specific groups of people under specific conditions, rather than findings that reveal only the net effects of the programs; when the values or standards used as evaluative measures mirror the standards that the members of the policy and program community use in assessing programs; and when cost and public sentiment are systematically incorporated into the evaluation.

In many ways, process or formative evaluations that have been directed by the intended users attend to the user's values. Systematically tested existing program variations have delivered findings that are more useful in selecting among alternatives, relative to much of the experimental work in evaluation that has been preoccupied with outcomes measures (Patton, 1988). However, attention to outcomes does not have to be synonymous with a value-free approach. Experimentally controlled studies, as noted earlier, can also incorporate the values of intended users and systematically review program variations. By incorporating these trigger mechanisms, the evaluation has a better chance of informing the selection of program alternatives.

Choosing an Alternative

Our discussion of the third stage of Kingdon's policy model refers to the use of evaluation in making decisions, or traditional instrumental use. In practice, these types of decisions are relatively rare. At the national level, they are very unusual; as we move down in scope to state and local program decisions, they become somewhat more common. Also, as we move from national policy to desk-level implementation, decisions in this stratified hierarchy can reinforce or, in many cases, undo the changes made at higher levels. In educational reforms, for example, state legislatures, state boards of education, state educational administrators, local boards and superintendents, principals, and teachers in the classroom all make choices that can prevent reform from being carried out (Cohen, 1995).

In many instances, nothing is done at all; no decision is reached. The Clinton administration's health care proposal is a recent example. No proposal had been around long enough for its tenets to soften-up the policy community. The public mood supported change, but there was no consensus on the type of program needed. Without consensus on a proposal, the policy window for change closed.

Decisions, whether federal in scope or affecting, say, a single community mental health board, are political. They can be informed, even guided by evaluation findings, but in few cases will the evaluation be the sole source of the decision. Our pluralist form of governing is open to much information and many values in making choices. Evaluations are unlikely to address all value considerations or to be the definitive source of information on all values. Evaluations, because of their independence and credibility, may more often serve to justify decisions already made on other grounds than to guide the original route to the decision (Majone, 1989).

Again, we can frame the expectations for use in the sensemaking and value positions that an evaluation embodies. First, as noted earlier, social policy and programming involve multiple layers of stakeholders, often with different ways of sensemaking (with respect to how they access and process information) and with different sets of values. Including these perspectives in the design and conduct of the evaluation increases the odds that the evaluation will be perceived as relevant and potentially useful to the various groups (Rog, 1985). Stakeholder views are pertinent in designing a number of aspects of the evaluation, such as in selecting what to study and measure (causal mechanisms and outcomes); choosing counterfactuals to provide convincing and persuasive evidence of the effects (or absence of effects) of the policy or intervention under study; and deciding over what period of time the effects should be monitored to inform decisions.

Use is likely to be enhanced not only by examining context and audience sensitivity, but also by carefully choosing the manner in which it is analyzed and presented. For ease of presentation, evaluation findings are often presented in the main—using measures of central tendency and staying at the molar, or macro, level. In some instances, when the findings are dramatic and relatively insensitive to individual differences, the molar level is adequate for directing action. In the evaluation of the nine-site homeless families program, for example, 85 percent or more of the families across and within the sites remained in their own housing eighteen months after receiving a housing subsidy and services (Rog and Gutman, 1997). This finding was particularly striking since the program served families who were considered multiproblem, had moved an average of every three months in the eighteen months prior to entering the program, and had long histories of homelessness and instability. The finding itself, because it was dramatic and consistent, motivated action. In the language of use, the finding was "actionable".

In many situations, however, data that can answer the familiar question, What works for whom under what conditions?, are sensitive to individual and site context differences that provide direction for specific action. As noted earlier, attention to context dependence makes the findings more generalizable. Explanation operates as a method for generalization.

Statistical methodologies (Rossi, 1997) that can examine the variable impact of interventions for different individuals, different time periods, different contexts, and so forth are tools the ER evaluator can use to increase the explanatory power of experimental studies. Multilevel modeling techniques (Bryk and Raudenbush, 1992) are useful in this regard. For example, in a multisite study of supportive housing, hierarchical linear modeling can model both consumer-level effects (such as the influence of ethnicity and severity of mental illness) and site-level effects (such as the amount of case management provided; whether housing is physically scattered or clustered; or the openness of the housing market).

Understanding the distributional impacts of a program emerges as a key generative mechanism in the sensemaking process involved in specifying program alternatives (this understanding also is critical in the alternative selection stage, described later). There may be interest, for example, in knowing not only the net effects of several different employment training approaches, but also if and how they have differential effects for individuals who are at varying places along the initial income distribution (see Friedlander and Robins, 1997).

Finally, use in this stage may be facilitated by understanding the processes that open and close policy windows. Knowing when and what types of decisions need to be made; the level of conflict in the decisions (Sabatier, 1987; 1988); and the different channels through which policy-makers receive their information (Weiss, 1988) can all influence how evaluation information is received.

Implementation Activities

Implementation of policy shifts the decision-making activity from higher policy levels to a local level, and, consequently, to the domain of local policy and program officials. Implementation decisions are generally more constrained that those at preceding stages, with the focus now on making decisions within the framework of a specific program or policy. The principal concern is not so much what to do, but how to do it. This is the exclusive focus of many practicing evaluators.

Local decision-makers have a variety of questions that evaluation can inform. Many of these questions are quite descriptive. What does the program look like in operation—in other words, who is it serving, and what activities are being implemented at what levels? In fact, realists have been interested in the descriptive elements for categorizing entities into *natural kinds,* which could be developed to include kinds of social programs (Bhaskar, 1975). Other questions warrant a more analytic investigation: How and why is the program in operation different from what was intended? How and why is the program changing over time? And finally, as in the previous policy stage, the question of impact—What is working for whom under what conditions?—continues to be a question providers and policy-makers have as they implement a policy or program.

To answer these implementation questions, a variety of evaluation activities can be used. Process evaluations (Scheirer, 1994) are intended to provide descriptive insight into the day-to-day activities of programs. Case studies (Yin, 1994) involving a host of qualitative and quantitative inquiries can provide insight into the how and why of a program, including attention to the broader context as well as the inner workings of a program. Evaluability assessment, a technique developed by Wholey (1979) to understand whether and how an outcome evaluation can be conducted, offers a method for analyzing a program's underlying logic in design as well as in operation. Activities such as performance measurement and monitoring (for example, see Newcomer, 1997), total quality management (Poister and Harris, 1997), and other types of routine monitoring and management information systems are also valuable in guiding implementation by providing detailed information on the administration and operation of a program. Finally, impact evaluations can also guide implementation conducted at various stages in an initiative to determine whether a program should be continued, changed, or eliminated.

As in the previous stages of the policy process, however, the ER perspective proposes that for utilization to occur, the evaluator should be cognizant of the context-specific generative mechanisms that relate to use of the data and findings. As in other stages, use involves an interplay between sensemaking and valuing, although during implementation it typically involves individuals intimately involved with the program's conduct. On one hand, during implementation, evaluation findings can generate the conditions for use because the problem has been framed, and one programmatic approach has been selected. There are typically fewer conflicting values (in other words, most of the people are committed to the solution to some extent because they are either involved in, responsible for, or interested in the program) and fewer decision-making levels. Therefore, the information produced can have a readily identified audience that is already interested in the initiative. Unlike other stages, the evaluator does not have such a diffuse and undetermined number of people who can influence decisions. Most typically, the evaluation activities have been commissioned by the program or others close to the program (for example, a foundation sponsor or government sponsor) who have some capacity to use the information.

On the other hand, there are barriers to use that the ER evaluator must recognize. For example, sensemaking processes of those closest to the program may rely on personal experience more than objective evidence. Successful cases with real names and faces, even if anomalies, can influence providers more than statistical evidence of failure or no difference. Often those most involved in programs, especially in service programs, come from a different community that places more value on subjective than on objective ways of knowing.

The ER evaluation perspective, as in the other stages of the policy process, incorporates this knowledge of the different sensemaking and valuing processes into how the evaluation activities are conducted. First, involving the program operators and officials in key stages of the evaluation process can help bridge their perspectives, cognitive processes, and interests with those of the evaluators. One way is through the facilitated development of logic models that portray the underlying logic and theory of a program. These models, as seen through the eyes of these stakeholders, inform the evaluator and tie the inquiry to the real experience and insights of those closest to the program. The process often elucidates the potential generative mechanisms that could be operating, and thus lays the groundwork for the measurement needed (for example, What measures should be tracked through a management information system or through focus groups in a process evaluation?).

The process of developing logic models as well as other aspects of the design also helps the program officials and others close to the program understand the thinking and processes of the evaluator. For example, in developing a management information system for a program serving homeless families, line staff as well as program directors and administrators were asked to take an active role in reviewing and reformulating the data collection instruments to be used with families. Many of the line staff initially had visceral reactions to the instruments—Why do we need to ask more questions of people who have been badgered by the system for so long? Why are we asking *these* questions? What is this for? The process of reviewing the purposes of the evaluation and how it might be used, and reviewing each question on the instrument, provided an opportunity to exchange ideas and communicate the values inherent in what was to be measured and for what purposes. Often the providers find that the divide is not as great as they had assumed; or if it is, they find that the process of communicating what they believe is important can inform and change the evaluation process.

It is equally, if not more, important to involve the beneficiaries of the program or policy in the process of designing and conducting evaluation activities to guide the implementation of the program. In broad initiatives, ER evaluation supports involving a slice of the public (for example, citizens in a community) through one or more vehicles (such as questionnaires, focus groups, or individual meetings) to help inform the data collection activities and the interpretation of outcomes. In other initiatives, direct beneficiaries and participants in the initiative can be involved in the process.

In a current initiative involving one of the authors, consumers of mental health services and housing help design and implement a set of process evaluations of supportive housing for individuals with mental illnesses, and these evaluations will be followed by a set of outcome studies. Among the mechanisms used are an ongoing panel of consumers who will review and comment on all key draft products and decisions of the evaluators (such as, initial designs and instruments); involvement of several consumers on a steering committee of project directors, housing officials, researchers, and others that directs the overall on-site study; focus groups of residents in the housing being evaluated; and direct interviews with consumers throughout the initiative.

Real involvement in the design and ongoing decision-making of stakeholders and potential users of the evaluation has been shown to be related to the perception that the information is useful (for example, see Rog, 1985). To be put into use, it may also be critical to provide the information in a way that relates to specific needs and interests. Net effect information, for example, helps with go-no go decisions but does not provide assistance with refining an initiative or retargeting its focus. Information at more molecular levels provides operators with more refined information on how a program works on the ground, with a level of specificity that may inform specific changes. For example, in case management reported through a management information system, reports were developed that showed the amount of time spent on case management with each family and the various types of activities provided (Rog and others, 1997). Not only was the system designed with the active involvement of the program operators and case managers, but also the reports used to provide ongoing information were designed with their input. Several sites struggled with how to use the average and range information on case management with families, until they helped us realize that the reports would be more useful if the unit of analysis was changed to case manager. Knowing how much time each case manager spent on various activities with the families they served provided more actionable information, since it paralleled how the managers viewed the implementation of case management through individual case managers.

Other barriers toward evaluation utilization in guiding the implementation of a program include time and resources. Typically, these competing demands within a program make it difficult for evaluation activities to get the attention and interest of stakeholders. Putting out fires, attending to crises, and meeting the other day-to-day challenges of a program or policy often feel all-consuming. These demands, together with a general lack of interest in evaluation, can make it difficult to mount an evaluation that has maximum likelihood of being useful. As for other steps, understanding the sensemaking processes of those involved and how the evaluation can best be shaped to provide information can help with crises and other challenges, and avoiding some of these problems may increase the relevance and usefulness of the evaluation activities.

Conclusion

To trigger use, an evaluation must provide findings that are actionable at a stage of the policy-making process that has an open window for action. It is rarely useful for an evaluation to report simply that a program is not working. Few programs are dropped, and few social problems disappear. Rather, programs are developed and changed, either through deliberate action or through evolution. Providing more explicit direction to those changes is a benefit of ER evaluation.

This underlines the importance of multiple sensemaking endeavors and values, as well as the marriage of multiplism with criticism. No single evaluation can incorporate the views of all those who may influence decisions about the program. No single evaluation can be definitive on all program issues for every stage of the policy process. If questions of importance are not answered by the evaluation that has been conducted, another evaluation may be needed. From a realist perspective, evaluations should be multifaceted and designed to answer questions as they become answerable and as (or hopefully just before) they surface in one of the policy-making streams. Rather than fruitlessly seeking to design the definitive evaluation, ER evaluators ask what type of evaluation will be useful for important audiences within the current program or policy context.

References

Bhaskar, R. A. *A Realist Theory of Science*. Leeds, England: Leeds Books, 1975.

Bryk, A. S., and Raudenbush, S. W., *Hierarchial Linear Models: Applications and Data Analysis Methods*. Newbury Park, Calif.: Sage, 1992.

Campbell, D. T. "Experiments as Arguments." In E. R. House, S. Mathison, J. A. Pearsoll, and H. Preskill (eds.), *Evaluation Studies Review Annual*, 1982, 7, 117–127.

Chelminsky, E. "On the Social Science Contribution to Governmental Decision-Making." *Science*, 1991, 254, 226–231.

Cohen, D. "What's Systematic in Systemic Reform?" *Education Researcher*, 1995, 24 (9), 25–30.

Davidson, R. H., and Oleszek, W. J. *Congress and Its Members*. Washington, D.C.: Congressional Quarterly, 1985.

Dunn, W. "The Two-Communities Metaphor and Models of Knowledge Use." *Knowledge*, 1980, 1, 515–536.

Elam, S. M., Rose, L. C., and Gallup, A. M. "The 28th Annual Phi Delta Kappa/Gallup Poll of the Public's Attitudes Toward the Public Schools." *Phi Delta Kappan*, 1996, 78 (1), 41–59.

Friedlander, D., and Robins, P. K. "The Distributional Impacts of Social" *Programs. Evaluation Review*, 1997, 21, 531–553.

Glazer, N. "How Social Problems are Born." *The Public Interest*, 1994, 115, 31–44.

Heclo, H. "Issue Networks and the Executive Establishment." In A. King (ed.), *The New American Political System*. Washington, D.C.: American Enterprise Institute, 1978.

Henry, G. "Community-Based Accountability: A Theory of Accountability and School Improvement." *Phi Delta Kappan*, 1996, 78 (1), 85–90.

Hilgartner, S., and Bosk, C. "The Rise and Fall of Social Problems: A Public Arenas Model." *American Journal of Sociology*, 1988, 94 (1), 53–78.

Kingdon, J. *Agendas, Alternatives, and Public Policies*. (2nd ed.) Boston: HarperCollins, 1995.

Lipsey, M. "Theory as Method: Small Theories of Treatments." In L. B. Sechrest and A.S.G. Scott (eds.), *Understanding Causes and Generalizing About Them*. New Directions for Program Evaluation, no. 57. San Francisco: Jossey-Bass, 1993.

Lipsey, M. "What Can You Build with Thousands of Bricks? Musings on the Cumulation of Knowledge in Program Evaluation." In D. J. Rog and D. Fournier (eds.), *Progress and Future Directions in Evaluations: Perspectives on Theory, Practice, and Methods*. New Directions for Evaluation, no. 76. San Francisco: Jossey-Bass, 1997.

Majone, G. *Evidence, Argument, and Persuasion in the Policy Process*. New Haven, Conn.: Yale University Press, 1989.

Mark, M. "Validity Typologies and the Logic and Practice of Quasi-Experiments." In W.M.K. Trochim (ed.), *Advances in Quasi-Experimental Design and Analysis.* San Francisco: Jossey-Bass, 1986.

Newcomer, K. E. (ed.). *Using Performance Measurement to Improve Public and Nonprofit Programs.* New Directions for Evaluation, no. 75. San Francisco: Jossey-Bass, 1997.

Patton, M. Q. "The Evaluator's Responsibility for Utilization." *Evaluation Practice,* 1988, *9,* 5–24.

Patton, M. Q. *Utilization Focused Evaluation: The New Century Text.* (3rd ed.) Newbury Park, Calif.: Sage, 1996.

Poister, T., and Harris, R. The Impact of TQM on Highway Maintenance: Benefit/Cost Implications. *Public Administration Review,* 1997, *57* (4), 294–302.

Popper, K. *In Search of a Better World.* New York: Routledge, 1994.

Portz, J. "Problem Definition and Policy Agendas: Shaping the Education Agenda in Boston." *Policy Studies Journal,* 1996, *24* (3), 371–386.

Rochefort, D., and Cobb, R. "Problem Definition, Agenda Access, and Policy Choice." *Policy Studies Journal,* 1984, *21* (1), 56–71.

Rog, D. J. "A Methodological Analysis of Evaluability Assessment." Doctoral dissertation, Vanderbilt University, Nashville, Tennessee, 1985.

Rog, D. J., and Gutman, M. A. "The Homeless Families Program: Results to Inform Policy and Program Change." In S. Isaacs and J. Knickman (eds.), *To Improve Health and Health Care: The Robert Wood Johnson Foundation Anthology.* San Francisco: Jossey-Bass, 1997.

Rog, D. J., and others. "Case Management in Practice: Lessons from the Evaluation of RWJ/HUD Homeless Families Program." *Journal of Prevention and Intervention in the Community,* 1997, *15,* 67–82.

Rog, D. J., "Implementation of the Homeless Families Program: Characteristics, Strengths, and Needs of Participant Families." *American Journal of Orthopsychiatry,* 1995, *65,* 514–528.

Rossi, P. "Perspectives on the Last Decade of Quantitative Applications in Evaluation." In D. J. Rog and D. Fournier (eds.), *Progress and Future Directions in Evaluation.* New Directions for Evaluation, no. 76. San Francisco: Jossey-Bass, 1997.

Sabatier, P. (1987). "Knowledge, Policy-Oriented Learning, and Policy Change." *Knowledge: Creation, Diffusion, Utilization,* 1997, *8,* 649–692.

Sabatier, P. "An Advocacy Coalition Framework of Policy Change and the Role of Policy-Oriented Learning Therein." *Policy Sciences,* 1998, *21,* 129–168.

Scheirer, M. A. "Designing and Using Process Evaluation." In J. Wholey, H. P. Hatry, and K. E. Newcomer (eds.), *Handbook of Practical Program Evaluation,* San Francisco: Jossey-Bass, 1994, 40–48.

Shulha, L. M., and Cousins, J. B. "Evaluation Use: Theory, Research, and Practice from 1986." *Evaluation Practice,* 1997, *18* (3), 195–208.

Weiss, C. H. "The Politicization of Evaluation Research." In C. H. Weiss (ed.), *Evaluating Action Programs: Readings in Social Action and Education.* Boston: Allyn and Bacon, 1972.

Weiss, C. H. "Where Politics and Evaluation Research Meet." *Evaluation,* 1973, *1,* 37–45.

Weiss, C. H. "Improving the Linkage Between Social Research and Public Policy." In L. E. Lynn (ed.), *Knowledge and Policy: The Uncertain Connection.* Washington., D.C.: National Academy of Sciences, 1977.

Weiss, C. H. "Evaluation for Decisions: Is Anybody There? Does Anybody Care?" *Evaluation Practice,* 1988, *9* (1), 5–19.

Weiss, C. H. "Theory-Based Evaluation: Why Aren't We Doing It?" New Directions for Evaluation, no. 76. San Francisco: Jossey-Bass, 1997.

Wholey, J. S. *Evaluation: Promise and Performance.* Washington, D.C.: Urban Institute, 1979.

Wingens, M. Toward a General Utilization Theory. *Knowledge: Creation, Diffusion, Utilization,* 1990, *12,* 27–42.

Wright, J. D., "Methodological Issues in Evaluating the National Health Care for the Homeless Program." In D. Rog (ed.), *Evaluation Programs for the Homeless.* New Directions for Program Evaluation, no. 52. San Francisco: Jossey-Bass, 1991.

Yin, R. K. *Case Study Research: Design and Methods.* Thousand Oaks, Calif.: Sage, 1994.

EPILOGUE: EXPERIENCE INFORMING THEORY SUPPORTING PRACTICE

George Julnes, Melvin M. Mark, Gary T. Henry

In the preceding chapters we have presented a wide range of ideas about evaluation that follow from a modern realist perspective. Taken together, these chapters summarize our response to the call by Shadish, Cook, and Leviton (1991) for more adequate theories of evaluation (for a fuller treatment, see Mark, Henry, and Julnes, in preparation). In addition to developing ERE in terms of the five components of evaluation theory that Shadish, Cook, and Leviton identify, we share their preference that a theory of evaluation be informed by lessons from experience. Such an openness to the lessons of experience is fundamental if evaluation is to reach its potential in informing social programming decisions. However, it appears difficult to sustain such a commitment to data guidance when it comes to evaluation theories (Chelimsky, 1997). Our analysis suggests that an important cause of this difficulty is the conceptual entanglement that results from framing evaluation debates in terms of controversies between the traditional paradigms of logical empiricism and radical constructivism. In addition to other failings, these paradigms appear to resist many of the lessons from experience. For example, too many of the dichotomies used to define the paradigms ring false with our practical experiences as evaluators.

Some readers of this volume might object that, for all of the talk about an emergent realist alternative, much of what we recommend is not that different from good contemporary practice by good evaluators. We accept this attitude, but have three responses. First, many evaluations do not meet the standard of "good contemporary evaluation by good evaluators," and we hope ERE will help others reach this level. Second, we attribute some readers' sense of familiarity with our message to the fact that realism is more widespread among evaluators and other social scientists than traditional rhetoric might suggest. Indeed, Baert (1996) expressed this view in criticizing the habit of some proponents of realism to claim uniqueness: "[Bhaskar's critical realism] is mistaken once it takes up a messianic role *vis-à-vis* the social sciences. . . .Many social scientists already follow realist principles anyway" (p. 521). Thus, when framed in contrast to logical empiricism or radical constructivism, most of us are realists of one stripe or another. Third, while we agree that many of the practice implications of ERE are not unique, we believe that ERE contributes some insights.

For example, ERE shares with traditional approaches to program theory (for example, Bickman, 1990) an interest in casual explanation. However, ERE adds specific emphases: (1) Given the stratified conception of reality, program theory can be addressed at multiple levels of molecularity; (2) understanding will often be enhanced if both more molar and more molecular analyses are conducted; but (3) choices about molecularity should be guided by utility.

Utility, however, need not be treated as a unidimensional concept (Weiss, 1997) or be viewed mechanistically. Emergent realism uses developmental concepts of assisted performance and scaffolding in its contentions that evaluation theory should support evaluation practice and evaluation practice should support social programs. From this developmental view, we join a variety of previous theorists in placing "the emphasis on the primacy of practice" (Putnam, 1995, p. 52). We believe this is best accomplished by understanding our natural sensemaking and valuing capacities, both as evaluators and as users of evaluation, and by developing theories that support them. We began this sourcebook with a chapter on practice, to highlight its primacy.

Our commitment to assisted performance in furthering development has important implications. One is that many current questions in the field, such as whether evaluators should report a range of findings, provide summative conclusions, or recommend specific actions, are misplaced when viewed as logical problems or as general principles. Instead, they are better viewed as developmental problems: Given a particular context, what sorts of evaluation processes and products provide constructive support for the various users of evaluations? Also implied by the developmental view is the notion of social betterment, which we embrace while we reject the positivist's view of progress. "We cannot prove that progress is possible, but our action is 'fantastic, directed to empty, imaginary ends' if we do not postulate the possibility of progress" (Putnam, 1990, p. 191). We offer emergent realism as a framework capable of supporting evaluation practice so that evaluation practice can in turn support social betterment.

References

Baert, P. "Realist Philosophy of the Social Sciences and Economics: A Critique." *Cambridge Journal of Economics,* 1996, *20,* 513–522.

Bickman, L. (ed.) *Advances in Program Theory.* New Directions for Program Evaluation, no. 47, San Francisco: Jossey-Bass, 1990.

Chelimsky, E. "A Plea for Integrating Empirical Results into the Theoretical Formulations of Evaluation." Plenary address at annual meeting of the American Evaluation Association, 1997.

Mark, M. M., Henry, G. T., and Julnes, G. "Evaluation, A Realist Approach: Monitoring, Classification, Causal Analysis, and Values Inquiry," in preparation.

Putnam, H. *Pragmatism.* Oxford, U.K.: Blackwell, 1995.

Putnam, H. *Realism with a Human Face.* Cambridge, Mass.: Harvard University Press, 1990.

Shadish, W. R., Cook, T. D., and Leviton, L. C., *Foundations of Program Evaluation: Theories of Practice.* Newbury Park, Calif.: Sage, 1991.

Weiss, C. "Do We Know Any More About Evaluation Use?" Plenary address at annual meeting of the American Evaluation Association, 1997.

INDEX

Ordering Information

New Directions for Evaluation is a series of paperback books that presents the latest techniques and procedures for conducting useful evaluation studies of all types of programs. Books in the series are published quarterly in Spring, Summer, Fall, and Winter and are available for purchase by subscription as well as by single copy.

Subscriptions cost $63.00 for individuals (a savings of 28 percent over single-copy prices) and $105.00 for institutions, agencies, and libraries. Please do not send institutional checks for personal subscriptions. Standing orders are accepted. Prices subject to change. (For subscriptions outside of North America, add $7.00 for shipping via surface mail or $25.00 for air mail. Orders must be prepaid in U.S. dollars by check drawn on a U.S. bank or charged to VISA, MasterCard, or American Express.)

Single copies cost $22.00 plus shipping (see below) when payment accompanies order. California, New Jersey, New York, and Washington, D.C., residents please include appropriate sales tax. Canadian residents add GST and any local taxes. Billed orders will be charged shipping and handling. No billed shipments to post office boxes. (Orders from outside North America must be prepaid in U.S. dollars by check drawn on a U.S. bank or charged to VISA, MasterCard, or American Express.)

Shipping (Single Copies Only): $30.00 and under, add $5.50; to $50.00, add $6.50; to $75.00, add $7.50; to $100, add $9.00; to $150.00, add $10.00.

Discounts for quantity orders are available. Please write to the address below for information.

All orders must include either the name of an individual or an official purchase order number. Please submit your order as follows:
    Subscriptions: specify series and year subscription is to begin
    Single copies: include individual title code (such as PE59)

Mail orders to:
    Jossey-Bass Publishers
    350 Sansome Street
    San Francisco, California 94104–1342

Phone subscription or single-copy orders toll-free at (888) 378–2537 or at (415) 433–1767 (toll call).

Fax orders toll-free to: (800) 605–2665.

For subscription sales outside of the United States, contact any international subscription agency or Jossey-Bass directly.

OTHER TITLES AVAILABLE IN THE
NEW DIRECTIONS FOR EVALUATION SERIES
Jennifer C. Greene, Gary T. Henry, Editors-in-Chief